The Mindset of Encouragement

How to: Lead with more power and less control

Nic Crisp

DEDICATION

Mum and Dad, this one is for you. For showing me
the power of both an intuitive heart and a rational,
logical mind.

"For to be free is not merely to cast off one's own chains, but to live in a way that respects and enhances the freedom of others"

Nelson Mandela

Contents

Preface

If you want to go fast, go alone. If you want to go far, go together.

African proverb.

Stepping up, and forward, individually and in alignment, has power.

We know that if we want to achieve anything with impact, we have to find a way to work together. We know that we are social creatures at heart, hard wired for connection. We know that creating anything meaningful and enduring requires a movement, followership and unity. When the energy for innovation and action is present, results can be swift and transformational. And at an individual level, whether we are personally oriented to making money to provide for our families, getting stuff done, making a difference in the world, being part of a community, or all of the above to some degree or other, the quality of the relationships we have with those around us matters. We know it. The belief in our interdependency is an essential foundation for the success of any system. The wisdom to know that we can't survive or get by alone, let alone achieve anything significant, has underpinned our survival as a species. Although the temptation can be high to forge ahead in a fit of desire and self-righteousness. To downplay the importance of bringing others with us; to take a short-term perspective, to go for a win, to take what we need (even if there is a cost to us somewhere down the line, or at someone else's expense). Within most organisations and teams this, the bigger picture—who and what really matters—is the part we can so easily lose sight of. We become endlessly creative in our ways to compensate in order to get our way or get one back. Descending into power plays found at the heart of all relational disconnect.

I have already introduced the word 'power' in two different ways. It comes from Latin, *potere*, and is defined as:

- The ability or capacity to act or do something effectively
- A specific capacity, aptitude or strength
- Strength, energy or force exerted or capable of being exerted

- Effectiveness at moving one's emotions or changing how one thinks
- The ability or official capacity to exercise authority and control

Power is associated with strength but is often interchangeably used with control. The ability to influence or direct the behaviour of oneself, others and the course of events. To have power over. Which can be used for the good or not, depending on the motivation, the intent – the "why" that sits underneath anything we do which has a transformative impact on the energy and results created by that action. Power can force, power can liberate. Having an awareness of our associations around this most important of concepts is an important one, what it means to all of us will be very different. As will the contexts in which we use it (or think we can use it) in terms of leading ourselves and others in the pursuit of making things happen within our organisations.

In this book I will look at power in ways that evoke freedom and connection. Power that encourages both ourselves, and others, to step forward, to have a voice, to give, create and work at our best, more of the time.

Power that encourages us:

- to lead with more confidence and presence
- to support those we work alongside to feel a greater sense of ownership
- to create a culture that facilitates and celebrates creativity and collaboration

I am a leadership consultant, exec coach and facilitator and this is the kind of work I love to do. Unlocking collective clarity, purpose and belief that makes incredible achievements possible. The kind that the leaders hope for, and can just as easily lose hope of, ever achieving.

Because leading change and large groups of people in an aligned way, is hard work and involves navigating some big tensions:

- How do we strike a balance between challenge—vital for fresh thinking and innovation—and alignment on the decision making required to make any of it happen?

- How do we keep a long-term perspective whilst also staying attuned and aware to what is happening in the here and now?
- How do we foster a sense of community, of belonging, whilst ensuring that disagreements where they happen are dealt with swiftly in the best interests of both the individual and the group?
- How do we encourage and invite feedback, especially the kind we don't like to hear? The lone voice of dissent who points out what the group has missed; the spark that dares to ask what if there is a different way? The mirror holder who reflects where we have delivered what we said we would and where we have not?

Tensions are conflicts—ones that we must welcome if we are to deepen our understanding, strengthen bonds, build trust and drive unified action. Navigating such tensions calls for consciousness, or awareness. But even when you have awareness, it is still not easy. We all make mistakes, say or do things with the very best of intentions in ways that fall short when viewed from the perspective of others (and sometimes we are capable of doing all of this without the good intent).

Which is why senior executives and their top teams will reach for someone like myself for an outside eye, for a little guidance. To help them see the things you often can't when you are part of the problem and/or the system. To learn.

I wrote a book a year ago called *Courage, dear heart. How to: look back learn and leap forward*. A book for leaders on the edge of change. It charts my own experience and those of the many clients I have coached in similar situations. The wake-up calls that come along to alert us that change is required, the creative ways we can employ to avoid what is staring us in the face, and the foundations for moving forward once we accept that change is inevitable. It is a book about alignment at a very personal level. Between what we say and what we do; what we stand for and how we show up; who we are and what we share with others. All of which are markers of integrity and trust, unlocking the kind of energy, purpose and joy that only comes from doing what we love.

This second book, *The Mindset of Encouragement,* is also about alignment at a collective rather than personal level and written for people who lead people. A practical guide for anyone wanting to lead with a lighter touch that has more power. Not the kind of power that comes from hierarchy, rank or titles. But the kind of power that comes from trust, alignment and responsiveness. It comes at a time when I am exploring professional partnerships myself to write, design and create alongside others, having worked for the last seven years very independently. As before, I intend to share my own insights and reflections alongside the very honest contributions of the clients I serve. I will share practical ways to support greater collaboration, communication and creativity both alongside and through others. And I will pose questions which will allow you, the reader, to think and reflect on what this may mean for you, your leadership and your organisation. Ultimately this is a book based on my own experience of leading teams over 25 years, the learnings shared by other teachers, mentors I surround myself with now, and the tools and techniques which I use as a consultant and share with the clients I serve.

I hold some beliefs about what drives success which sit at the heart of this book:

Trust

Trust is the foundation. An awareness of how trust can be built and lost—how when present, this most intangible of assets is worth its weight in gold. Knowing that people give more, create more, stay longer, and spend more. It matters not whether you are looking at employees, customers or suppliers: trust has a multiplier effect when it comes to both inputs and outputs. Service, productivity and profitability are on average higher in companies with high trust scores. Where the people working in such organisations are happier, clearer and more connected to each other and their reason for existing.

Alignment

Know who you are. Through greater awareness and understanding, particularly of the organisational culture, its origins and history. Of the people that make it what it is, how they show up on the inside with each other and on the outside to customers and consumers. To members of the public who call on their services and stakeholders operating in their legislative, environmental, political and competitive contexts. Alignment only comes from a willingness to listen, notice, observe both what is said and not said, but undeniably there. To hold oneself and others in alignment, clear on who we are, what we stand for, and how this links to what we say and do.

Responsiveness

Go with what is there. Having an awareness of the tensions at play and the ability to move with fluidity and agility. To not get fixed in one style of leadership, or indeed one mode of thinking, doing or behaving if that is not what the context or the team is calling for (or indeed, what is working).

Simplicity

Less is more. Simplicity supports good open and honest two-way communication. It helps us to take in, interpret and take action. The frameworks I use are simple and they work, which is what matters.

Realness

Realness has depth. Story telling has resonance when spoken with raw honesty, as it reminds us that we are not alone with the challenges, thoughts and experiences we face. Sharing also builds collective learning. Through practical experience, trial and error, which is the very essence of all innovative and creative practice. I hope some of the real stories and the insights contained within them serve to inspire and ignite a desire to seek out ways to make the relationships you have at work stronger, and the results you dare hope for that much more likely.

Encouragement

Be 'for' others. We all have the capacity to simply tell others what to do (usually with an edge of frustration) or to employ the even more short-term strategy of doing it for them. The word encouragement means to give confidence or hope, to inspire with words or behaviour, and refers to any action designed to make something more likely to happen. It is derived from the old French *corage*, meaning to give heart to another. As a mindset it is enabling and supportive, designed to liberate others to think and act with freedom and confidence. Fostering independence, not dependency.

This is my intention for this book, and my work.

And with that in mind, let's go......

Chapter 1: The heart of the issue (process vs. people)

"If I had an hour to solve a problem, I'd spend 55 minutes thinking about the problem and five minutes thinking about solutions."

'

Einstein

So, what's the problem *you* want to solve?

Let's start here. Whenever I get a call to work with an organisation, they will tell me what they need.

"I would like you to come in and facilitate a session so we can work on refining our strategy/values."

"We need to work on our innovation process, it's not clear who does what, who passes the baton to whom."

"Can you run a session so that we can talk about roles and responsibilities and work out our new structure."

They tell me the solution. Often what they want to address are perfectly legitimate requirements that they have failed to come to an agreement on. But the issue underpinning them is often that the people involved are not talking to each other effectively, if at all. If they were, the issue would probably have been worked out long ago. And the trouble is if you focus on the presenting issue, which is sales speak for the thing that people first cite when they are asked to expand on their current dissatisfaction, they will come up with the thing that is front of mind, the most recent issue that has presented itself. They can also tend to focus on the first solution that comes to mind too. The easiest thing, in their mind, to fix.

And the go-to for many leaders is process and structure which, let's be honest, is far easier to control than people.

"If everyone was clear on what they were supposed to be doing we would all be ok," is the predominant thought-process. Which is a very rational assumption, and of course clarity generally helps people move together in an aligned way. However, if you have ever worked in an organisation that restructures every 18 months only to find itself in the same position of restructuring when the next HRD or Board Director gets appointed then you will know very well the down sides that often come with it. Confusion, disengagement, loss of talent, knowledge and expertise, a fall in productivity. Not to mention the advantage you hand to the competition and the opportunity cost, all the things you could have done but didn't because the organisation was on hold, looking inward, waiting for things to be clear. Now, of course, it all depends on your purpose for downsizing, but it can be the most dreadful and costly waste of energy if you are reorganising to get rid of the people you haven't performance managed. Particularly for those that stay.

"What's the point?" said one client who called me after I had written the above paragraph. "I could stress myself about it, but there is not much I can do, other than wait it out until we get through consultation." In the waiting it out, energy tends to be spent on keeping business as usual ticking over. Anything that requires effort or risk will be put on hold. Which tends not to be good foundations for success or market leadership.

The problem with jumping in too quickly with a rational solution, like fixing a process or changing reporting lines, spans of control, job roles and responsibilities, is that if the issue was to do with the people concerned then you have just implemented a solution, just not one for the problem you have. A bit like moving chairs on the Titanic. Something that can end up costing you more in terms of frustration and apathy of the more astute around the senior team (and those looking up at them) who can see the underlying issue exactly for what it is.

I have worked with other teams recently guilty of jumping to process first:

The first team asked me in to help them clean up their innovation process. Too many projects going through too many steps, with too much detail being demanded too early on, was frustrating the innovation team who wanted more space up front to create unique products. It had become a bit 'us vs. them' with the technical and supply chain teams, who were equally fed up with having their part of the process crashed right at the end in an effort to meet the demands, high standards and deadlines of the customer. When I first met them, pretty much everyone was feeling frustrated, not least their board director who was exasperated that all he was hearing was noise and that no one seemed to be able to suggest anything to make the noise go away. "If we need to get them all in a room to change this process Nic, then that is what we need to do. What I don't want though is a load of moaning. I want solutions."

I was always taught that the thing to remember about process is that its only purpose is to make the outcome, and importantly the behaviour you want, more likely to happen with ease, simplicity and pace. It is a facilitator. The role of process is not to make things as difficult as possible but that is exactly how it can feel if you have ever had to raise a PO or an IT query when someone decided in the interests of cost that it would be a really good idea to outsource the function. Often what happens when processes are created is that the content owners in their functional silo say what they want/need in splendid isolation of everything and everyone else in the system, not least those they are there to serve.

The pivot point for change came when I asked the team to talk me through their innovation process end to end. At each of the 6 steps of their process, I asked the same question: "So what is the purpose of this stage?" And each time there was a bit of a tumbleweed moment, as though I had asked them something they had never considered. Because in reality they hadn't—at least not together. And in the dialogue that followed, involving some considerable debate, they aligned on why they were doing it in less than 5 words. The exercise was a revelation. The supply chain teams at the end of the process had no idea there were 6 stages at all, or what was being discussed at the start. Once the cross functional leads had their purpose clear then the actions they were forcing in too early in the process became really obvious, as were the people who needed to be present to input their perspective and/or expertise to make decisions that could relieve pressure further down the line. The issue here wasn't the process, although it was easy to blame. The real issue was that at each stage, and for the process overall, the context had not been clearly stated. In essence, why we are doing this? and what matters most? This team were brilliant activators, great at spinning a lot of plates and very adept at coming together in a crisis to make things happen. They were not so great at stopping every now and then to regroup, reflect and ask some big questions, which include learning from their successes and mistakes before running into the next project. The review step was missing from their process entirely, not on paper, but certainly in practice. This is not uncommon, particularly where the success of the team, as it was for this one, is based on its ability to do. But every strength does indeed have its shadow, its downside. One that I can relate to. If I look back, I spent most of my twenties operating like that. An activator, brilliant at getting stuff done, not prone to too much reflection. I had to adapt fast when I started to lead people, as being great at doing lots of stuff myself wasn't going to get me very far. My purpose had to change, and with it my mindset and behaviour.

When we lose sight of why we are doing what we are doing, and when our purpose is not aligned, conflicts will naturally arise. In this situation people will generally assume what they are doing is right and carry on doing it over, and over, again. That's how silos and siloed thinking emerges. Each function does its part, then when you add in huge amounts of activity which is neither visible nor joined up, it places stress on individuals to cover the cracks. Good people will always find a way, which you can rely on to a point. Until things go badly wrong, which they almost inevitably will when you do too much, for too long. This is where the wake-up calls will tend to magnify, and you end up with each function pointing the finger at the other. When given an outlet to express their frustration they will cite all the over and above work they have had to do to get the end customer served. Whilst it is easy to place blame on another part of the system that is at fault, what is often true is that everyone in the system feels equally hard done by, over-worked, unappreciated, and all are left wondering why on earth they bother.

Getting this team to collectively step back to take in the big picture meant they were more quickly able to land on the decisions required at each stage. As their perspective changed, so did what was important. As one head of function said, the purpose of this process is to support us to make really good decisions. In part he was right. And it is people who make decisions, not the process. Something that can only be achieved through dialogue, which is the one behaviour they most needed to practice.

I have worked with many great HR professionals over the years overcoming people issues and if you ask them, they will tell you that:

- The most frequently cited reason people leave a company is that they don't get on with their boss.
- Most grievances and tribunals would never happen if people had only communicated more openly and honestly (or sought help to do so) earlier in the process.
- The greatest internal challenge facing most organisations whether they are driven by profit or not, is engagement.
- The most common issues they observe at Board level is the lack of alignment between colleagues and peers.
- The biggest grievance they themselves have is that they are viewed as Human Resources Police; a reactive, process driven function. Not valued as a discipline or as equals to their commercial or operational colleagues. And their complaint would appear to have some credibility when you think that the role of HR Director / Chief People Officer according to KPMG is not represented on the Board of

about 20 % of the top 100 companies in the UK. And that is the top 100, which suggests that the number is only going to get worse as you go down from there.

What all these issues come down to is our ability to connect and relate to each other:

- Am I valued?
- Do I have a say in how things happen around here?
- Can I trust you?

Relational issues or disconnect happens where one party stops being able to communicate openly, and honestly, with the other.

Disengagement happens where the answer to one of the above questions is no (and over time we don't address it).

We will come back to why this happens and some of the watch outs that can occur in cultures as they evolve. But wherever an individual or group does not feel heard or seen there will generally be an issue. It is just one of those fundamental, universal and basic human needs we all have, and something which has to happen on a regular basis rather than a once a year exercise when you ask people to speak up and complete an anonymous on-line survey, from which leaders are frantically, and often individually, sent off to create action plans to put whatever has been flagged as wrong, right.

When presented with any issue, before we jump into analysis or solutions, it is really important to be clear about the consequence. The so what. If there isn't much of one then you might have an issue, but not one that is worth time or energy solving. You might choose for example to just give it time to work itself out. It is surprising how many things do when given time. But if the consequence for the organisation or the people operating within it is significant, and one that it or they cannot continue to bear, then that is a different matter entirely.

We are all free to choose who we work for. People tend to move employer every 5 years in the UK according to Insurance firm LV (which matches official statistics in the USA) vs. the traditional job for life we may have expected to have 40 or 50 years ago. For an organisation to continually evolve, some movement is generally a good thing for all concerned. However, if you have ever left a company or job you loved purely because of the behaviours of the person you reported into then you will know the meaning of regrettable loss. The kind of ending that leaves a lingering resentment long after a new opportunity has presented itself. For those who leave and those who remain.

The average tribunal in the UK costs £8,500 according to the Chamber of Commerce. Anyone who has ever had to spend time preparing for a tribunal or attending one to give evidence will know the cost in terms of stress placed on all parties. It is a measure of last resort, an important one to have to protect the rights of individuals and principles of fairness but, much like a divorce, you want to have exhausted all other consultative options before you get to that point for the interests and well-being of all concerned. Whether that be financial or emotional.

Engagement can be directly measured as a human cost (prolonged periods of stress, anxiety, disconnect and apathy can affect our mental and physical health, not to mention the impact it has when we take this stress out on those we love and care for outside of work). But there is also of course an opportunity cost at a collective level when it comes to results, innovation and competitive advantage.

The opportunity cost is all the stuff you aren't doing because people are either burned out (flitting between too many priorities and doing none of them justice) or have checked out (and doing just enough to keep themselves out of trouble). Unless of course it has got to the point where employees are taking to social media or other public platforms to air their grievances in which case disengagement can also cost you your reputation and future business.

Internal in-fighting of course also has a cost in terms of time, money, wasted effort and stress. It takes far longer to do what needs to be done. Projects, initiatives, ideas do not progress at all simply because people get entrenched. It becomes personal. I've watched those kinds of spats play out at senior level. And although it pains me to say it, I've been a player in one with someone I worked alongside but did not respect. I'm sure you have too. The principle of cabinet responsibility is a good one, if only people could actually live by it without all the power games, complaining, avoiding, counter-briefing, saying one thing and doing another that actually goes on, draining trust, momentum and results in the process.

The consequences of relational issues play out as costs, that can be financial, reputational, legal and/or emotional. The trick is to understand just how much drag relational issues place on both the energy of the individuals concerned, the collective purpose and outcomes they are there to deliver. And if left to play out how costly these incrementally become for the organisation, other employees and the sum of their collective action and investment.

In other words what does or does not happen as a result of individuals in a team, or teams in their silos, locking horns or checking out?

Reflection Exercise 1

If anything, I have covered thus far provokes any recognition, then I invite you to take the time to reflect on the organisation or team you are currently a part of:

What are the issues you see that stop your team or organisation being successful?

When did they start?

What is the consequence of these issues continuing to play out?

Chapter 2: Organisational mindset (power vs. control)

"Problems can't be solved with the same level of consciousness that created them in the first place."

Einstein

If you know you have a repeat issue that keeps coming back around, no matter how many times you attempt with good intention to solve it, then it is usually a good idea to look a little deeper at what is really going on and why. From a rational perspective i.e. looking at what is getting done or not done; the outcomes and results being achieved; the repeat failures and gaps; how things work in the organisation like processes, structures and language—all very visible, tangible and hard manifestations of the system and what it is there to do.

It is equally, and I would say more, important to have an eye on the emotional; what goes on in the minds of the people who work, lead, interact within the organisation and how this impacts the behaviour of the group when it comes together. This is what Edgar Shine calls the invisible forces of culture, and is made up of 2 levels:

Values: what we believe is good and right in the organisation, the principles that guide how the organisation achieves its goals.

Core beliefs: our assumptions that, whether we are aware of them or not, ultimately decide how we act, how we show up to others and how we shape our organisations and our world.

The combination of rational *and* the emotional drives what we see, create, do and deliver. But it is the invisible which manifests the visible. Whilst it is so tempting to keep tinkering about with the obvious stuff that can be changed and controlled in the name of transformation, it is actually what goes on in the minds of the people that will ultimately determine what gets done and how. Real transformation comes from a change in perspective, not process. But in order to shift perspective, of course, it is fundamental to be aware of what the current belief system is and where it came from. In other words, what it was in our history that set in motion a particular behaviour?

This principle is as relevant for organisations as it is individuals. We all have a back-story that is unique to each of us; values and beliefs that developed or were instilled in us by our primary care givers that shape who we are, how we relate to others and the world around us. Just as every family has its own dynamics, stories that are talked about, a few secrets that are not, patterns that seem to transcend time, so of course do the organisations and the groups in which we work.

Looking more deeply at this question, at what lies beneath, unconsciously driving the results we see on the surface provides an awareness of the patterns, the beliefs and the past events that continue to shape us now. Awareness opens a space for curiosity. To look at what helps and what may hinder both our present and our future. It also facilitates a choice between that which we hold on to (because it is sacred, the core of our success) and of course, conversely, what we choose to let go of (because it gets in the way or is no longer needed).

So, as an anchor point, I would like to reference the work of renowned consultant Frederic Laloux. In his book *Reinventing Organisations,* he looks at the way humans have organised themselves over time, and the shifts in consciousness, or in other words, perception, that created new models for how we work. There is a great saying that we all stand on the shoulders of giants, and he has built on work by a great many philosophers, psychologists and historians who have explored the shifts in the development of humanity over the past 100,000 years. Work which has illustrated how, at each stage, there has been a corresponding leap forward in our abilities, our way of thinking, and what I think is interesting in the context of a study of leadership development, in how we collaborate, create and communicate. In essence, humans have invented ways to organise themselves which were inextricably linked to the prevailing worldview. What is more interesting is that the legacy of all of these stages still exist in organisations today, providing some profound insight on not just how our organisations work, but why, and what it might take to transform their development for any leader truly invested in revolution, or at the very least an evolution to maximise the organisation's strengths and minimise the drag of its downsides.

In the following, I have attempted to headline the work of Laloux who simplified each of these stages of human development and attributed them colours as a means of then matching them to the organisations that emerged in their image.

I have created a summary of these stages, available as a PDF from my website (more on this at the end of the chapter). As you read each one, see if any of the insights resonate. What I found interesting is that whilst we have developed tremendously over time, it is surprising in some ways, that how much of the way we relate to each other has not.

Stage 1: Impulsive Red

Through the earliest development stage of humanity (100,000-50,000 BC) we organised ourselves in family groups of no more than 30-ish people, which is about the maximum a group can handle without too much complexity and conflict. By 15,000 BC humanity evolved to slightly larger groups of about 100 people and as tribes formed, so did the concept of eldership: leaders who by virtue of their experience and wisdom commanded special status and authority. Fast forward another 5,000 years and we start to see the first chiefdoms ruling not just hundreds, but tens of thousands of people. The world at this stage is a hostile, dangerous place. The purpose is survival and with it comes a replaying drama of conflict, violence and domination—in essence, a pattern driven by the need for power in its rawest form, where slavery is common.

Organisations moulded in Red consciousness still exist and the behaviours are built on a very simple foundation of control which can be described as 'my way or the highway'; power over, wielded with the use of extreme violence and intimidation to keep others in line. Organised crime, prison culture, street gangs, civil war zones are all examples of where this model still plays out. Where the chief will only remain the chief if they can demonstrate total domination of the group. The moment their status as the biggest silverback in the room is in doubt, they become vulnerable to the next pretender. So in order to drive some stability in what is a very hostile environment, what you tend to see in Red organisations is a chief surrounded by family members, or those whose loyalty has been bought in some way and often extreme and highly visible displays of punishment to keep others in their place. All in all, a pretty stressful, highly charged, unpredictable environment in which you tend to find frequent bursts of infighting for survival and to keep ones' place in the pecking order.

I have not worked in cultures operating from a Red paradigm, but I have encountered leaders with this mindset and have had tales regaled by clients of leaders they have worked for who demonstrate some, if not all, of the tell-tale signs. Leaders who thankfully stopped short of violence, but who frequently engaged in aggressive and demeaning outbursts. I have once observed a senior leadership team whose only collective time together used to be at the weekly Monday meeting, where the Chief would operate a kind of creeping death approach to facilitation, firing questions at each individual, demanding an update that was entirely for his benefit, in an atmosphere that was tense, aggressive and entirely devoid of any collective dialogue or creativity. Everyone dreaded coming in and said as little as possible, until it was their turn to be drilled. At best the purpose appeared to be to get out unscathed, to update in a way that did not provoke an adverse reaction. But frequently, of course, he did blow up and when he did, the team would meekly take their dressing down. Reinforcing his belief that they weren't capable, and theirs that he was a volatile bully.

I have also heard of one or two leaders who have broken boundaries physically and emotionally. As one client put it, "I once saw him throw a glass of water in the face of his CEO at dinner. We all just sat there as if nothing had happened. Not saying anything made it ok, but it wasn't ok."

And another who sat in a meeting whilst a colleague was yelled at and demeaned. "It's a bit like domestic violence Nic. If this is tolerable, then that is tolerable, and you start to wonder where is the line? I regret not saying anything. I should have intervened."

What holds this kind of behaviour in place is fear, a code of silence. Once broken, so too is the illusion of power held by the leader, which can mean a hard fall for them when it comes and liberation for all of those in their shadow. A great recent example being Harvey Weinstein. Interestingly it was the people who knew it was happening and said nothing who came under as much scrutiny as Weinstein himself.

Stage 2: Conformist Amber

Humankind moved to what development psychologists call the age of conformity when we moved from tribes to civilisations, states, bureaucracies and organised religions. The dominant preoccupation in this paradigm is fitting in, and whereas Red is very individualistic in its purpose and reactive in its behaviour ("I want it my way and I want it now"), Amber has a more collective focus of 'us vs. them'. In essence, if you are a member of a group who think 'our way' then you are saved, but if you belong to a different group or culture who don't think or look like us, then you are looked down on (or worse still, damned). Amber societies have explicit or implicit codes which govern how others should look, think and behave; a concept of morality and group norms that are set by a role in authority. Whilst Red is based on a principle of ultimate control in the hands of one person that is, in reality, pretty fragile, Amber is much more about control in the hands of an institution which drives for order, longevity, predictability.

Stability of course has its advantages, facilitating a longer-term perspective and more ambitious infrastructure or social projects which might take decades or even centuries to finish. With a mindset of stability, the concept of a repeatable process and a highly organised structure becomes more important. A structure purposed to finding ways to replicate the same outcome over, and over, again, irrespective of the people in each role. Which means, in essence, that for Amber organisations people are viewed as replaceable. What matters is the enduring survival of the system. But given that order and predictability sit at the heart of this worldview and the systems enduring success, change tends to not come easily when the context shifts and demands a new way of thinking or working. And the organisations can even be guilty of covering people issues up to preserve the illusion of status quo and reverence for the system itself. The cover up of systemic abuse in the Catholic Church being a prime example.

The rule of Pontificial Secrecy designed to protect sensitive information between the Vatican and its leaders allowed church officials to hide, deny and avoid facing up to the consequences of on-going and historical abuse and point-blank refuse to cooperate with either state investigating authorities or victims. This rule was lifted in 2019 after the weight of evidence and thousands of cases brought against the Church worldwide finally pushed the institution into action. Tangible demonstrations of transparency and the clearing out of unacceptable attitudes and people, including leaders who knowingly covered up abuse for so many decades, may take longer to manifest. But every change requires a first step and this one, taken from the top, is a start.

Another interesting facet of organisations built on a Conformist Amber perspective is given that the underlying motivation is about control, they will often drive for domination, becoming the monopoly in their sector and can therefore be slow and inflexible in their response to the advent of competition or swift changes in the context in which they sit.

This drive for control of course shows up on the inside of the organisation through more rigid cascading top down in traditional pyramid reporting structures and a plethora of policies and rules to control how people work. Planning and execution, the what and the how, are distinct with both tending to be the responsibility of those at the top, and the doing relegated to those at the bottom. Reward comes through the use of promotions, titles, ranks, uniforms. Given that conformity is the name of the game here, to get on you have to fit in. What is interesting is that what you often find is the predominant underlying belief system of 'us vs. them' will almost inevitably show up in the mindset of the people operating within these organisations - bosses vs. employee, head office vs. frontline, employee vs. employee based on affiliation to a union for example, or where one has one set of terms and conditions that is different to the other (non-uniformed vs. uniformed in the Fire Service or Police, for example).

'Us vs. them' also can also show up in the clear division of roles and responsibilities aiming to keep people in their lane. Any consciously imposed division based on structure or mindset will almost inevitably give way to silos. And given that the underlying motivation within these organisations is for control, and the endurance of system, Amber organisations have a tendency to try to process their way out of any divisions that emerge, loading more red tape, policies and procedures to make people in the organisation 'do what they are supposed to'.

The upside of these very stable highly predictable cultures is that they are able to lock in people who strongly identify with the social ambitions of the organisation. There is a glue that holds together people and relationships aligned to service, loyalty, duty and obligation. They tend to be very paternalistic in nature and if you think of our public institutions, the NHS, education system, military, our emergency services and civil service, they will have the scale to offer both the breadth and opportunity that can last a lifetime and an identity (not to mention a family, which is their often underplayed strength) which can be a hard one to leave when your 30 years is up.

I have worked with a number of organisations that orient towards Amber conformist principles. I have seen the frustrating levels of over-processing and an attitude of compliance that can prevent upward challenge when most needed, bewildering level of over paternalistic caretaking from company owned housing, gold star pension schemes and talent 'bench' systems. The latter being something I have only ever seen in public sector organisations and those that were privatised in the 80's. The bench exists for people who are moved out of roles because they have not got the required skills, experience or capability. Rather than being managed out of the organisation, they are instead kept in a pool, doing project work until a hiring manager has a vacancy which matches their capabilities. This is a practice that is very well intentioned (to retain talent) but in reality, is both desperately inefficient and encourages under performance, whether that be in capability or attitude, to be carried and passed on to someone else in the system rather than dealt with. Alongside some of the most highly sophisticated performance and governance frameworks, I have seen the lowest confidence and capability to have open and honest performance conversations, the highest number of grievances and a talent pool that largely moves between one institution to another. But for all the downsides, the people I have met in those organisations are some of the most genuinely service driven, altruistic people I have had the privilege to work alongside. And when an emergency situation occurs, in the form of a worldwide pandemic like no other we have faced in living memory, it is these public institutions and the people who serve within them who together stepped up to provide a unifying force to keep us safe that galvanised a genuine sense of communal pride and gratitude in return. Stability and order certainly have their place. Particularly when events, and the environment we find ourselves in, are somewhat chaotic.

Stage 3: Orange Achievement

If the worldview of Amber is order, Orange is in essence 'what if?'

Orange questioned authority, challenged thinking and the status quo and sought to understand how things worked so that they could be improved. Pioneered by artists and scientists during the Age of Enlightenment and the Renaissance, it was the Industrial Revolution and the huge leaps forward in science, technology and innovation over the past 30–40 years that really defines this stage of human development. However, as with both of the previous stages, Orange Achievement also brought great benefits and a few glaring, unintended consequences. On the upside, huge progress, prosperity and the potential for instant communication anywhere in the Globe and with it over consumption, a throw away materialistic culture and an unprecedented level of destruction of the world's natural resources and the eco system on which we all depend.

Achievement, innovation and money really are the drivers when it comes to the organisations that thrived in line with Orange thinking and most of the top global branded companies of today are reflective of this stage of human development. Goal oriented, founded on a belief that anything with the requisite effort and application is possible and that the more money, more consumption, more material success we have, the better we, and the world, will be.

In terms of structure, the basic hierarchical pyramid still exists with some level of freedom within the framework for project teams and cross-functional collaboration in pursuit of innovation to exist. Interestingly it is the domain of leadership that defines the biggest shift from Amber organisations, in the move from command and control to predict and control. The leadership role in these organisations moves from defining how things get done to setting the strategic framework and providing greater freedom for employees to define, challenge and create how best to achieve the objectives set. Control still exists to ensure success and delivery of the goals but comes in the form of talent management and the range of HR led processes and practices like performance frameworks, succession planning, incentives and bonus structures, signalling a shift from stick to carrot. Control however remains a core issue with this paradigm. And whilst Orange thinking places far greater emphasis and trust in the talent and innovative capability of the individuals operating within the organisation, leaders at the top can often in practice find it far more difficult to give up control, continuing to hold and make decisions which would be far better left to those working for them.

Clarity around who gets to decide, and on what, is critical for Orange organisations. As a leader once said to me a very long time ago when I first started working in one, "People don't actually mind not having the power to make a decision, they at least know where they stand. What they do mind is being told they have decision-making authority only to find, in practice, they do not." That in reality, everything has to go up for the approval, or decisions are made and then frustratingly overturned by someone higher up the chain. Decision-making is one of the areas of fundamental disconnect and breakdown for Orange organisations that is the least talked about and one that I spend most time supporting leadership teams to work through. Alongside facilitating open and honest conversations, which is a prerequisite for good decision-making and a topic we will come back to. The permission to challenge the status quo and come up with new ideas is a key tenet of Orange thinking, and all successful organisations built on this paradigm. However, it can stand and fall on the perceived openness of the senior leadership team. In other words, can we really say what we think? Or can we challenge thinking provided that it marries with the views held by those more senior— those who hold the power to grant promotions and rewards? When the balance tips towards the latter, then you tend to see a lot of upward manoeuvring amongst ambitious individuals and a stifling of the diversity of thinking which is actually this paradigm's shining strength.

Another defining characteristic of Orange thinking, influenced by the industrial revolution of their inception, is that they tend to view organisations through a very rational logical engineering perspective, that the organisation is a machine. Strategic imperatives, operational efficiency and effectiveness, flawless execution, marginal gains, KPIs, balanced scorecards and business transformation are highly prized. The purpose of the organisation to drive to achieve ever more challenging goals; to do more, more quickly, in the pursuit of year on year growth and a healthy shareholder return. Little wonder maybe that 51% of CEOs of the UK's largest companies come from a finance and accountancy background.

What generally attracts people to working within this kind of system is money and recognition for being highly competent. In a meritocracy, put the work in and do well and you will be rewarded with promotions, titles, bonuses, shares. For the individuals leading these organisations the rewards can indeed be great, leading to some condemnation for the fat cat salaries and bonus structures. Those which can, and have, encouraged questionable finance and accounting practices, pension scandals, misuse of personal data and the abuse of suppliers all in the name of desire to make the numbers look good (BHS, Tesco, Google and Facebook being fairly recent examples). It is this desire and the dark side of Orange thinking that exposes its real vulnerability and potential for seemingly untouchable giants to tumble like a house of cards.

Desire as a mind-set, generally speaking, does not like the word no. It rejects limits and instead relentlessly pursues and drives for more, more, more—with scant regard for the cost, the risk or the downside. It spins plates with an arrogance that it cannot fail and rejects any suggestion that it might. Until of course it does.

We witnessed the consequence of this mindset during the banking collapse of 2008 that triggered world recession, the bankruptcy of Lehmann brothers and the close shaves experienced by Merrill Lynch, AIG, Freddie Mac, Fannie Mae, HBOS, Royal Bank of Scotland, Bradford & Bingley, Fortis, Hypo and Alliance & Leicester. The latter who would have gone the same way were it not for the government bailouts that year. Over-leveraged, they crumbled under the weight of bad debt, driven by a combination of deregulation of the financial markets and the behaviour of bank executives who thought they were untouchable. No limits in the form of compliance checks and balances meant that the mindset of desire could flourish unbounded, with bonuses encouraging and rewarding the behaviour which was ultimately responsible for its downfall. Greed was indeed good.

In 2010 Andy Haldane, the chief economist of the Bank of England, estimated that the total cost of the crash in foregone economic growth was between $60 trillion and $200 trillion, or between one and five times the planet's GDP. "To call these numbers 'astronomical' would be to do astronomy a disservice," he said.

There was indeed a huge cost felt for the next decade, a price ultimately paid for by the UK taxpayers, who were also asked to take the hit when, 10 years later, construction giant Carillion collapsed after going into compulsory liquidation. The May 2018 report of a Parliamentary inquiry by the Business and the Work and Pensions Select Committees said Carillion's collapse was 'a story of recklessness, hubris and greed' and accused its directors of misrepresenting the financial realities of the business.

"This morning a series of delusional characters maintained that everything was hunky dory until it all went suddenly and unforeseeably wrong. We heard variously that this was the fault of the Bank of England, the foreign exchange markets, advisers, Brexit, the snap election, investors, suppliers, the construction industry, the business culture of the Middle East and professional designers of concrete beams. Everything we have seen points the fingers in another direction–to the people who built a giant company on sand in a desperate dash for cash."

In other words, the directors sought to blame everyone else around them rather than look at the part they may well have played in bringing about the organisation's downfall. This kind of denial, or arrogance, is also symptomatic of a mindset of desire. Grounded, aware leaders look inside, those running on desire will always point the finger outside of themselves when everything goes wrong.

This is not to say that all organisations led with an Orange perspective are inherently bad, far from it. The brand led innovators of our time have made our lives easier, connected us globally in ways our parent's generation could never have imagined. We are for the most part richer, living longer, travelling further; working more flexibly thanks to the huge advances in science and technology in particular, with brands to cater for every conceivable human need and occasion. Are we happier? That is maybe another question and our experience of getting back to basics during lockdown may forever change what we see as priorities and how we balance our lives, and love, of work and home.

But these failures highlight the importance of leading from the core strength of this model, encouraging upward challenge, innovation, seeking truth and holding leaders accountable. For leaders this means being open to challenge. Ensuring there are sufficient people in and around the organisation who are prepared to hold the mirror up, to keep themselves and other leaders honest about what works and what does not, and in their integrity with the impact they have on society.

As I write, the outcome of the impact of Covid-19 is unclear but we are already starting to hear a number of big names clamouring for government bailouts to shore up fragile business models. If there were underlying problems with cash flow and an over reliance on debt before this crisis, then a halt in revenues, spending and confidence as unprecedented as this one will surely expose more big names—not limited to the airline industry and the already beleaguered high street retail, drinks and hospitality markets. As a commentator on Radio 4 said, as the crisis hit in March 2020, "Consumers don't mind a bail out but what they do expect to see is a change in behaviour of those leading these companies."

The truth is behaviour and the outcomes that behaviours drive, can only change when our mindset changes. And sometimes sadly it takes an almighty wake-up call in the form of a catastrophic collapse or a virus that humans have not found a way to control to provide another shake out and shake up that in time opens a door for real transformation to take place. On the latter we shall see.

Stage 4: Green Pluralistic

If the Orange paradigm's guiding metaphor is the machine, Green would be family. Where one prizes the rational and what works, the other is more concerned with the emotional and how people feel. One is purposed to drive commercial gain, the other fairness for all. Green thinking emerged during the industrial revolution by a small group of activists campaigning for the abolition of slavery, women's right to vote, democracy and equality.

'Not what is right for me or my tribe or my religion, but what is right fair and just for all human beings regardless of race, sex, caste or creed.'

Fairness, community and consensus sit at the heart of the belief system of the Green paradigm. Which show themselves in leadership that favours listening to the perspective of others, empathy and being of service. There is a sense of nobility, of higher purpose and idealism based on the greater good for all. In short: We not I.

Organisations based on a Pluralistic Green perspective tend to reject the notion of traditional power structures and hierarchy. Decision-making is conducted by consensus and, where possible, pushed down to the lowest levels. Leaders in these organisations are chosen on their ability to give up rather than retain a tight grip on control and to adopt what Laloux calls a servant style of leadership, one oriented to empowerment, development, listening and trust. In essence, rather than promote highly competent functional specialists, strategic thinkers and problem solvers who tend to rise quickly in Orange organisations (whether they can lead people or not), what Green values more in its leaders is the ability to build relationships and get the best out of people. Feedback is a crucial component of evaluating leadership performance, a practice often extended to recruitment with employees taking part in the interview process to choose their leaders.

I remember years ago being told about a company from Finland whose revolution in leadership (and the company's fortunes) came when all employees were invited to a large conference room and asked to go stand behind the leader they wanted to work for. Anyone who was a competent contributor but who had no people lined up behind them were made individual specialists, highly prized for the technical skills and experience they brought, with line management removed from their responsibilities. Those who had a huge following held leadership positions devoted to coaching and development of those in their care. However uncomfortable the thought of this highly visible (and exposing) process might appear, I'm sure you can all think of someone you have worked for who, given the opportunity, you would have not chosen to line up behind. Someone who may have been viewed by the Executive team as top talent for their intellect, technical skills and/or ability to manage up rather than connect across and down. Bravery, a belief in doing what is right, and using resources for the good of all sits at the heart of this paradigm and facilitates some innovative practices when it comes to people.

Another key identifier of Green Pluralistic organisations is the importance placed in shared values and culture over process as the determining driver of behaviour. It is fair to say that most companies I work with have company values. Ask leaders to talk about what they are and what they mean in practice, you soon get a feel for whether they truly sit at the heart of what they do, or not.

"Do you have values?" I asked one Chief Exec of a charity, in our first meeting to talk about his strategy. "Yes, we did some work on that a couple of years ago. I will have to send you them as I can't remember what they are." He did some work with his team to generate company values, they couldn't decide so he decided for them. But once on the strategy document they went nowhere, unsurprising maybe as they were not owned, nor were they designed to be. I later did some work with his senior team to capture the history of their fairly new but rapidly growing organisation. As this team openly shared their stories there were some incredible turning points of innovation and a great deal of raw emotion and pride in the importance of the work that their fundraising supported. As it turned out they did indeed have values, but not the ones on the original power point slide.

On this point, I saw an address that Brian Chesky CEO from Airbnb had made to Stanford University. In it he said, "Integrity, honesty–those aren't core values, those are values that everyone should have. But there have to be like three, five, six things that are unique to you. And you can probably think about this in your life. What is different about you, that every single other person, if you could only tell them three or four things, you would want them to know about you."

I loved his reference. It is quite true that most companies have some pretty bland words which all look pretty much the same when you line them up. Making values real is an exercise I have done many times for senior leaders stepping up and forward into big new challenges and, for some, changes in direction both individually and collectively. If ever there is a time to anchor into who we are it is at the times we are tested and when we are called to sell ourselves to others. Authenticity being a winning strategy for both, building trust at very intuitive levels. We feel its resonance. But whatever reason your reason for taking a closer look at your values make them real and resolutely you, even down to how you qualify them.

A great example of this came from an organisation I have worked alongside called Anixter. 45 years ago, the founders of this organisation presented their beliefs and business style in a blue book, which this global systems company still gives to every new starter today. Here are a couple of the organisation's values by way of illustration, found in the well-used version I was given by one of its senior leaders:

Truth – We tell the whole story not just part of it. We don't stretch it, bend it or avoid it. And if someone raises hell when you tell the truth let them. Just say it like it is. One little lie and you are a liar.

Express yourself – Think! Think often, think hard, and then say what you think. Feel! Have strong feelings then express them. And don't get mad when others do.

Enthusiasm – Enthusiasm is the greatest business asset in the world. It beats money, power and influence. Enthusiasm is contagious so carry it in your attitude and manner. It will increase productivity and it will bring joy and satisfaction to our people. Enthusiasm brings results.

What I love most is the clarity of voice and energy which blasts off the page. The way these values are articulated says a lot about who they are, as does the pride which leaders within this organisation have of their Blue Book. If this is an exercise you would welcome doing at a very personal level, then read chapter 7 of *Courage, dear heart*. It can be an easier exercise to do for a company when we have taken the time to look inside ourselves.

Green organisations root themselves in these strengths, ensuring values are clearly lived and role modelled from the very top, not merely espoused on the odd poster. They are consciously chosen to define what the organisation cares about and are inextricably linked to its purpose; in other words, why it exists and for whom. In fact, leaders operating from this paradigm see the focus on people and culture as their primary responsibility, which elevates the role of HR and the genuine care extended to stakeholders both inside and outside the organisation. Something which then very obviously shows up in the practices, service promise, the consumer, customer, supplier experience. The way they balance a purpose to deliver shareholder return with one that seeks to give back, to positively impact wider society and the communities and environment in which they operate.

A really good live example of this is Pret, who at the beginning of the Covid-19 outbreak in March 2020 placed the following ad across all social media: "Dear NHS workers, your hot drinks are on the house from today and we'll take 50% off everything else. Thank you for everything you are doing. We look forward to serving you. With love, everyone at Pret." Whilst this was undoubtedly a nice marketing gesture, copied by many retailers in the weeks that followed, it came from the company that shows itself to be consistently innovative, swift to make decisions, commercially successful and purposeful. Pret describes its mission to serve good coffee, make all its food fresh on premise each day 'whilst trying to do the right thing'. The Pret foundation, set up by its founders in 1995, runs alongside its core business, aiming to alleviate poverty and hunger. The organisation works with grass roots charities to give all unsold food to the homeless rather than mindlessly binning it as most restaurant chains and food retailers do. A powerful symbol of We not I.

Organisations built on Green principles can just as easily be found in both commercial and not for profit sectors, but what they all have in common is leadership that is 'for others'. The difference being when they tend to act from their heart, their higher purpose, rather than being an opportunist stunt or words that look good on a poster, you intuitively get the feeling they actually mean it.

As marketing and advertising giant BBH said in a Marketing Briefing in March 2020, "In the past we have seen lots of companies with the best brilliant intentions, but the intentions were poorly executed. This is not the time to be beating your own chest. This is the time to be a good corporate citizen. To contribute to the public good, and not to be 'seen as' a super good company."

I would say the difference is indeed in the intention. Do you have a purpose to do good (from the heart) or a desire to be seen as good (which comes from ego)? Does the intention come with generosity for others? Or to exploit a situation for oneself?

A good example of this was gifted to us all through the actions of the Sports Direct boss Mike Ashley who first lobbied to make his business an essential supplier and put his prices up on all products as we went into lockdown which prompted his first PR backlash, then furloughed his employees whilst telling them to work so that they could deliver online, thus invalidating the terms of the scheme.

A genuinely purposeful intention always shines through. There are many examples of organisations who turned their factories over to making hand sanitiser, PPE equipment and ventilators. Excel and the NEC whose exhibition centres were converted as back up for the NHS would also be a good illustration of the genuine good (and truly exceptional creativity) that can come when leaders respond from a Green paradigm. The payback for their efforts will come in time. But speaking to leaders I work alongside within organisations at the forefront of vaccine development and emergency response, they are already noticing the massive engagement boost with employees, proud to have played a pivotal leadership role, not to mention the genuine admiration from stakeholders from the outside.

Stage 5: Teal Evolutionary

Laloux describes this final stage as being the latest evolution in our development. One that, as with all of the others, has always been there. Teal thinking is the foundation of all Eastern spiritual philosophies and lies at the heart of indigenous tribal belief systems. A stage of development that prizes the wisdom and power within each of us, that centres on a reverence for Mother Nature, the inter connectedness of all living things and living in alignment with what is; the present, letting go of all notions of control over how we think things 'should' be.

People who work and lead in organisations operating from Teal thinking have captured and applied this sense of spirituality. Whilst this can be a challenging concept to embrace in a corporate context, what it means in practice is leading through intuition and inclusivity, influencing rather than controlling, reading the context, seeing what emerges from the collective intelligence of the organisation as a whole and through the building of interconnected, flexible teams and networks. But again, taking the essence of spiritual practice and applying it to drive new thinking and implementable solutions in an inclusive way is something that many leaders may have experience of without realising it.

As an illustration, these are 4 laws from the Hindu faith:

The first one says: *the person who arrives is the right person.*

No one enters our life by chance. All people around us, all those who interact with us, are there for a reason, to teach us and help us progress.

The second law says: *what happened is the only thing that could have happened.*

Nothing, absolutely nothing that happened in our life, could have been otherwise. That's how we learn the lesson and we move forward. Each of the situations that occur in our life is ideal, even if our ego is reluctant to accept it.

The third one says: *whenever it starts is the right time.*

Everything starts at the right time, not before nor later. When we're ready to start something new in our life, then it will take place.

The fourth and last: *when something ends, it's over.*

That's it ... let it go. Nothing is permanent. Learn from it and move on. Be enriched by the experience and evolve.

When I posted these on my work social media an ex-colleague got in touch to say he had never made the connection until that point that they were in fact directly correlated to the principles of open space facilitation, which are:

- Whoever comes are the right people
- Whenever it starts is the right time

- Whatever happens is the only thing that could have
- When it's over, it's over
- If you find yourself in the position when you are not learning or contributing, move somewhere you can

Open Space is a technique used by innovation specialists and facilitators to surface the collective intelligence from a large group – i.e. where there is a problem you want to solve or an idea you would like to build on harnessing the talent, perspective and experience of others. The unique differentiator with Open Space is that as a facilitator or problem owner you do not seek to control who goes in what group, or which problem or question they work on. Participants are encouraged to follow their own energy, to contribute to the aspects of the opportunity or issue being discussed that they are most engaged in solving. If they want to leave at any point to contribute to a different discussion they can. This is the law of two feet: that if you are neither contributing nor learning then it is your responsibility to respectfully find somewhere you can. A condition explicitly set for the group that directly highlights the importance of both passion and responsibility as the basis for creating the very best result.

I was first trained in these techniques over 20 years ago; back then the purpose was to create new product propositions for drinks brands. I went on to use them as I moved into senior executive leadership roles to co-create strategies, to lead engagement and value creation sessions. As a consultant, I use Open Space still as a perfect format for a wide range of contexts including strategic direction setting, visioning, conflict resolution, stakeholder/employee consultation and engagement.

A couple of years ago when I retrained in open space techniques with Toke Moeller and his team of European facilitators, I was invited to work alongside the Secretary General for the World Conference of Religions for Peace, Bill Vendley. He, with leaders from the Vatican, Hindu, Buddhist, Muslim, and Jewish faiths had come together at a European Forum with about 5,000 delegates from around the world as part of an initiative called Ethics in Action: to join in conversation to support more sustainable development and peace in the world. I am not someone who is in any way religious. As a facilitator, attachment to the content of the discussion is not required (and can, in truth, help enormously) but it was one of those sessions that has stayed with me.

To kick off the session Bill told a story of a chance meeting with a cameraman in an airport in Sierra Leone, the cameraman had been sent there to capture stories of peace emerging from conflict but did not have money for a visa. Bill agreed to pay the cameraman's visa if he agreed to photograph religious leaders who were acting as mediators between two groups. As they began their trip Bill noticed the cameraman was filming not the leaders, but stories of loss, hope, faith, resilience, strength of the ordinary people both impacted by the fighting and those who were recruited as fighters as children. This unlocked an insight for him, "Peace is not the absence of war but is a gift of reality, rising confidence and hope."

Many of the group taking part in the event went on to share personal examples of times they had a similar revelation, experienced the impact of engaging in conversation to really listen to others, particularly those chance encounters we have, and the empathy and sense of connection this brings.

That session led by Bill turned out to be a masterful illustration of authentic, engaging and intuitive leadership – with a personal presence that was truly captivating, humble and exceptional. The training also practically served to teach me how open space can powerfully work in a group of several hundred people.

Listening and learning for the purpose of continuous improvement is key to Teal thinking, which includes what happens when one of the 4 laws are not observed—when control or a sense of obligation and duty pervades and overwhelms the willingness to trust, let go and see where the energy in the room truly lies.

I had been asked to work alongside a Chief Exec to see how the development and communication of a new strategy had landed with the senior team below, to assess the level of alignment in the what, how and why, and facilitate the group to fill in any of the gaps. Five platforms had been identified; I asked the team to go stand by the one they felt most personally motivated to solve. Four flip charts filled quickly, one remained empty. Which was feedback in itself; here was a platform which they had been told to explore but which in truth they didn't want to. One of the Senior Executives stepped in to say he would own it and after a rather elongated pause a few others joined him. When it came to articulating one clear idea and action from the session, two groups struggled. One which had been taken over by the person whose 'job' it was. He shared his summary, which, from the reaction written all over the faces of his colleagues, was a little different to what the group had actually discussed. The second to struggle was the group working on the platform no one had any true energy for. In an effort to control the outcome, they missed the opportunity to tune into what was really being said. The group would have been better off discussing what would need to change for them to want to work on it, or how they were going to say no. As it was, compliance won, and the result was poorer for it.

And it is this principle that Teal captures. So, if the metaphor for Amber is order, Orange is a machine, and Green is family, then Teal would be a living organism. A concept that is in some ways reassuringly familiar. How all living things and nature works, but one that radically challenges traditional organisational structures, practices and culture in that the very essence of it is fluid and adaptable.

Teal thinking accepts and supports the wisdom that people will always find a way. It lets go of power and control, distributing information openly and transparently (whether this be in relation to financial performance or pay) and decision making specifically, from being in the hands of a few at the very top. Rather than operating from an "I decide" paradigm of Amber and Orange or of the "we decide" consensus favoured by Green, it shifts to a "you decide" model where decision making is pushed down to those who are closest to the detail, activity and value creation for the customer. There is still one decision maker (or problem owner) but these people own the decision rather than pushing them all up to the top. Which in itself allows for far greater freedom and responsibility.

What lies at the heart of this shift are the assumptions these organisations hold about people, both explicitly and implicitly.

Firstly, Teal consciousness is based on a desire for what Laloux calls wholeness, or in other words, authenticity. A belief that when we bring who we really are to work we tend to be happier, more productive, more purposeful. This is in direct opposition to a mindset that differentiates the 'work me' and the 'home me', or in any way places demands on what we have to do or be seen to do in order to fit in or get on. I have to say, having coached now for as long as I have, I have heard those words many times over. Expressed as a longing to work in a culture where my clients could just be themselves, work less hours and from home more, lose the guilt of juggling kids and work and the dread in the pit of their stomach that they are just about holding it together but doing neither justice. I also hear the extensive list of all they would do and often, more importantly, what they would say if they knew they could not fail. Or more accurately what they would say if they did not think they would be judged poorly for it. Flexible contracts that allow leaders to pick their kids up from school or work from home 2 days a week so they can avoid sitting on the floor of a train to London for two hours a day, or three or four day weeks for those at senior levels. Quite small, simple adjustments which can feel like a big deal, and make a huge difference to those who have the courage to ask for them. In Teal organisations, these are not big asks.

Teal organisations welcome the whole self, not just the part we bring out for show. Maybe this too will prove to be another benefit to emerge from lockdown and endless Zoom calls where leaders have for the first time got to see what each other's houses and spare rooms look like, what books they have on the shelf or the stories behind the virtual backgrounds they choose. They will have shared the inevitable joys and disruption of home schooling, children and teenagers wandering into the study demanding attention, food or mediation to resolve sibling spats. This unique time with so many of us working from home has been a great leveller and an experiment that many leaders and companies had previously resisted; perhaps through fear of what not being seen would do to their perceived commitment, perhaps through lack of trust of what people would do if left to their own devices. This situation has forced organisations and individuals to confront those fears and let go. It will be interesting to see how many of us want to go back to the way things were.

So, this is a paradigm which values realness over status, titles, hierarchy, ego, presenteeism and politics. One that is driven by trust rather than fear. And one which, crucially, supports both individuals and the organisation as a whole to feel, be and do better, in alignment. Which includes balance between our home and work lives and an appreciation and support for individuals' health and emotional wellbeing and development.

One client of mine who recently resigned from a very traditional, paternalistic organisation to work for a consultancy was shocked to find her new employers talking about support for women going through the menopause as an example of their wellbeing package. "No one can bring themselves to talk about feelings here let alone women's problems," she said jokingly. But the truth is, part of what sold her is that this was a place where she could both shine and feel safe, where she would not have to hide who she was or what she was going through outside of work.

In this way, the paternalistic 'bosses know best, workers need to be told what to do, when to do it and how' moves to a more adult to adult relationship built on trust and a belief that people are inherently good (rather than lazy), can be trusted (rather than need to be monitored and controlled). That there can be no high performance without happiness (it's not all about money) and that real insight and value is created by those closest to the customer (rather than those who sit at the very top). It also has an underpinning belief in the power of teamwork and prioritises practices, structures and reward mechanisms that support teams (rather than individuals) to create, deliver, learn and grow.

This belief in turn determines the defining visible difference in the way power is held. Traditional hierarchical pyramid structures in these organisations simply do not exist and are replaced by self-managing teams and networks.

Power is given to the group to decide how best it should work. Managerial roles are eliminated in their entirety replaced by coaches, mediators and facilitators who have no profit and loss responsibility or management authority. Their purpose being to facilitate the group to think, create, resolve conflict, reflect and improve performance, available to drop in and support both individuals and the group in the event of the team not being able to work out an issue itself.

Meetings happen as the situation demands it, purposed to making decisions and creating workable solutions (not to meet because it is what we do on a Monday every week, or to meet and defer decisions to other meetings where the people with the real power get to decide what happens next).

This gives the organisation a fluidity to create structures to resolve problems as they emerge rather than being bound by structures that leave leaders running from one fixed monthly meeting to the next with no time to think or do the work that will deliver the numbers they endlessly report, present, analyse and discuss. It also puts paid to the rather pointless and protracted negotiations that tend to happen during traditional planning processes. Where sales teams are given responsibility to do a bottom up, only to be told they have to hit a number that someone at the top has decided is required. In most cases where this happens in Amber or Orange organisations, the power held at the top wins and everyone signs up, unwillingly or at the very least resentfully, to a number they either don't really believe in or indeed, have no plans to deliver. Unless they have been sandbagging, deliberately holding back on what they commit to in the first few rounds of planning so that they can come in at year end above target with ease. I used to work with a sales director well known for this practice. No one trusted him as far as they could throw him, but he was a nice guy just playing a game, which of course the system rewarded him handsomely for. The downside of such practices is that employees stop doing what is right for the company and instead look to do what is good for them (spending budgets before year end so that their budgets aren't cut the year after is another classic). In Teal organisations realness dispenses with games, pretence and farcical processes, and trust empowers greater truth telling when it comes to what can be achieved, what assumptions underpin these ambitions. When you set no targets, employees are simply encouraged to do the very best they can.

A culture that prizes balance, awareness, connection, fluidity and trust works very differently in all aspects relating to control: structures, processes, targets and people.

HR processes and policies are minimised, with administration of key ones like succession planning, pay and reward delegated down to the responsibility of the team. They decide who joins, who stays and leaves the team, how roles and people are reallocated to best suit the needs of the organisation. Individual performance calibration is undertaken by peers, who tend to be more challenging in reality with more recent and tangible data to draw on, rather than by those one or two levels up (who may not know the individual at all outside of their contribution at one or two meetings, and therefore only see the individual when they are 'on show'). Recognition for high performance is awarded to teams rather than individuals, which supports the very behaviour that this structure depends on (and that most traditional Amber and Orange organisations can struggle with for differing reasons). Support functions like IT, Finance, HR, Compliance, Quality and Safety are kept to a bare minimum and where they do exist, experts are held in the organisation to provide guidelines and advice but have no decision-making authority. This keeps boundaries clear and silos minimised with decision making the responsibility of the operating teams, provided that advice is sought out by all those whose input will support the team to make the best possible decision. The expertise is highly valued, but purposed, less to making rules for others to follow and more to supporting front end teams to flourish.

In his book, Laloux describes in detail organisations he has studied from around the world in diverse fields of healthcare to consultancy, manufacturing, energy and teaching who all operate from this new paradigm. He also makes the link that whilst organisations built on Teal thinking might sound a tad new age for many of us who have grown up in traditional structures and hierarchies, they are not so innovative when looking through the lens of our school leavers. Kids who have grown up with a mobile phone, iPad and laptop since primary age with instant access to an online world which is largely unregulated, unstructured and founded on principles that are not dissimilar to those underpinning Teal thinking:

- No one can kill a good idea
- Everyone can pitch in
- Anyone can lead
- No one can dictate

- You get to choose your cause
- You can easily build on top of what others have done
- You don't have to put up with bullies and tyrants
- Agitators don't get marginalised
- Excellence usually wins (and mediocrity doesn't)
- Passion killing policies get reversed
- Great contributions get recognised and celebrated

(source: G Hamel)

So as with all innovation, what seems impossibly futuristic now may just turn out to be what our grandchildren take for granted. We shall see. But it is clear that the much talked about Millennials and Generation Z do think and behave in very different ways to the 40 and 50 somethings found leading most large organisations. Whilst it is never wise to make sweeping generalisations that apply to all people, it is true that our societies are becoming more open, literally and metaphorically, and our children are experiencing the world in very different ways than we or our parents did. It makes sense to see how our perceptions, values, beliefs, attitudes could be shaped by the time we came into the world, as much as it is possible for them to be developed by our interactions and experiences over time.

Dr Alexis Abramson, an expert in generation cohorts, has attributed characteristics to the terms so freely banded about. If it helps, here is a short summary of each:

The Silent Generation

This is the first defined generational group referring to those born between 1926 and 1945. These people grew up in a recession, lived through the aftermath of two World Wars, and the name attributed to them comes from an article in Time magazine from the 1950s, alluding to the shadow of a Victorian upbringing where children were taught to be seen but not heard. There is a strong backbone and sense of fortitude found in this generation who Dr Abramson describes as:

- disciplined

- value-oriented and loyal
- interested in direct face-to-face communication

Baby Boomers

This term refers to the generation that were born in the years after World War II and was attributed by the US Census Bureau. This group captures those born during the population surge between 1946 and 1964, when the birth rate began to decline again. Boomers, certainly in the UK post war years, grew up experiencing lack (rationing, recession and energy restrictions) but were more rebellious than their parents' generation, craving freedom as society started to become much more progressive in relation to sex, sexual orientation and class. They are wealthier, having benefited from the housing boom which Millennials now struggle to access, and now, as pensioners are far more active.

- committed
- self-sufficient
- competitive

Generation X

The Resolution Foundation thinktank defines Generation X as those born between 1966 and 1980. They grew up in a time when technology was advancing fast, but it wasn't nearly as readily available as it is today. This generation straddles both the digital and non-digital world and can appreciate the importance of both. They were the first 'latch key kids' growing up in households where, for the first time, both parents worked. They have also been described as the sandwich generation, now supporting both older parents (who are living longer than their grandparents) alongside their own children (who are in education and living at home far longer than they themselves may have done). They experienced divorce at unprecedented levels, financially they tend to have higher levels of debt than previous generations and expect to work far longer before retirement. Dr Abramson describes them as:

- resourceful
- logical
- good problem-solvers

Millennials (Generation Y)

This cohort refers to those born between 1980 to 1995, a term introduced by Howe and Strauss about the generation to come of age at the turn of the Millennium. They're often described somewhat ungenerously as lazy and entitled, generation 'me' on account of their confidence and optimism (and reported higher levels of narcissism). They have higher expectations, tend to be more environmentally aware and more challenging of brands, politicians and leaders who do not share their ideals and values. They may be the first cohort since the Silent Generation to achieve less economic success than their parents. They are also the first generation to have lived in an online world, where anything you want to know, you google:

- confident
- curious
- questioning of authority

Generation Z

This generation starts at around the Millennium and are the babies of Gen X. They are young, leaving college and university into the world of work having never known a life without smart technology (the iPhone launched in 2007 as they were primary age). They are more aware of issues concerning body image, cyber bullying and mental health than previous generations. Having grown up during the global financial crash and ensuing recession, there is a suggestion that they may be much more driven to save and make money. Something which can start well before the age at which they are legally allowed to work using their own online brands, supported by platforms like Depop. They are described as:

- ambitious
- digital natives
- confident

Marrying these cohort values and drivers with the organisational paradigms, it is possible to see how one might support the other. The values and motivations of the Silent Generation fit well with Amber principles, those underpinning the Baby Boomers and Generation X align well to the Orange paradigm, Millennials to values of Pluralistic Green. What Generation Z, and the new Generation Alpha who are growing up behind them, value as they start to lead within our organisations we shall see. But it is easy to see how one can challenge and drive change in the other, particularly in terms of the societal, environmental and ethical impacts that younger generations care significantly more about from the institutions, organisations and brands they choose to interact with. Millennials and Generation Z certainly place more value on travel, experiences and wellbeing alongside any requirement to make money. Changing priorities require more flexibility, more fluidity, more focus on the quality of one's life, and the impact our work has on the communities in which we live. Something which can also come back around in later life, once the focus on achievement through promotions and money has run its course. Or has been found wanting. I know that this is how I have come to work in the way I do.

As my friend and colleague Emma Gunton said to me at one of our vision days together: "Nic you spend your time supporting leaders to create a strategy, but you don't have one." Made me smile. It is true is that I work to the principles of Open Space. I trust that those who are drawn to work with me will be the right people, that the creative partnerships I have are with people I trust, where there is alignment in our values. I create a vision for my life as a whole, for the challenges and travel I want to experience, the time I want to set aside to be with my girls and the creative projects I feel passionate about. But I set no targets, and over the past 8 years a constant flow of meaningful work, interesting clients in diverse fields and opportunities for growth have always come, often at exactly the right time. I also know many other leaders who have come to work in the same way, particularly those who have become disillusioned over time with the constraints of working in Orange organisations enough to leave, and to create their own businesses in the model that fits their values, principles, strengths and lives.

As one client said to me in the research phase for this book, *"The first organisation I worked in for many years was highly successful, very formal, with very clear set expectations. I moved to work for another which was very dictatorial, 'I'm telling you to do it, you had better listen.' The current company I work for is smaller, 500 employees, led by a bunch of entrepreneurs helping one another and learning together. Eveybody is doing stuff outside of their skill set, pushing boundaries, so we have to give feedback and solicit help. Work becomes a perpetual conversation figuring out how to do it, its very honest and direct, purposed around how we work on making things better. In my twenties I was just so happy to get a job, it was all about the money and the car. What I have realised is how important it is to look at the culture, who my boss is, to look at the office space and see if it feels a happy, welcoming, place to work. I have learned to do my due diligence. To use the interview process to see if this is a culture I want to be a part of."*

It is an insight I have heard retold many times. Underpinned by a change of attitude that is less 'Am I good enough for them?' and more 'Is this culture right for me?'

And when we feel this deep sense of alignment, that we have found our place, our people, doing work we love, I think it is truly possible to know the meaning of success. Which rarely has anything to do with titles, ranks, grades, or even—despite what we may think at times—pay.

For now, I hope the outline of each of the organisational paradigms has provided some food for thought.

Looking more deeply at what lies beneath, unconsciously driving the results we see on the surface provides an awareness of the patterns, the beliefs and the past events that continue to shape us now. Awareness opens a space for curiosity. To look at what helps and what may hinder both our present and our future. It also facilitates a choice between that which we hold on to (because it is sacred, the core of our success) and of course, conversely, what we choose to let go of (because it gets in the way or is no longer needed).

This is the essence of responsiveness.

Reflection Exercise 2

Should it be helpful, I have created a one-page summary of the key stages of development from Red to Teal. This is available as a PDF on my website:

https://headandheartleadership.co.uk/organisation al-mindset/

For now, when reflecting on these organisational paradigms, their values, beliefs, structures and mechanisms for reward and decision making:

Which most closely represent the one you are a part of now?

What strengths do you identify with?   What downsides do you experience?

What if anything would you want to be different in the future, and why?

Chapter 3: Leadership, culture and the 'say do' gap

"There is nothing inherently better about being at a higher level of development, just as an adolescent is not better than a toddler. However, the fact remains that an adolescent is able to do more because he or she can think in more sophisticated ways than a toddler. Any level of development is ok. The question is whether that level of development is a good fit for the task at hand."

Nick Petrie

I read a really interesting article by Esther Perel, relationship therapist, author and speaker. In it she shared an achingly simple diagnosis, that under any relational disconnect you will usually find one or more of three dynamics has been compromised:

- **Power and control** - *Do I have a say in what happens around here?*
- **Care and closeness** - *Do you care about me? Do you have my back?*
- **Respect and recognition** - *Am I valued? Does my contribution matter?*

It always stuck with me, as all great insight does, for its truth and clarity. It speaks to where disconnect may be playing out but of course also points to the obvious aspects which require attention for relational connection and engagement.

Put very simply I think:

How do we choose to agree to get things done in large groups and how do we choose to relate to each other as we go about it? Attention to the doing and being. One cannot work without consciousness of the other.

What is interesting in terms of the history of human and organisational development outlined in the previous chapter is how these relate to the core themes which repeat.

Who has power and control?

This is one of the defining characteristics. Particularly when it comes to the sharing of information and decision making.

- Does it sit at the top or is it shared?
- Do we hold it back or give it away freely?
- Who do we involve in which decisions?
- How as a group do we decide?
- How do we manage conflict in the event of us not being able to decide?
- Do we defer decisions, push them up, endlessly circle and prevaricate?
- Or do we make quick, clear decisions in the knowledge that some might be wrong (but we can always learn, adapt and change)?

What do we care about?

At a strategic level, where do we focus our energy, and what is our vision of success? Money, service, growth, making the world a better place, building stronger communities, people, customers, being first, the biggest, the only? If we care about some or all of these things, in what order do we care about them?

- When we say something is important, how do we show that we really mean it?
- When the pressure is on, what comes first and what gives?
- What is the balance between our agenda and those of others?
- Are we here to give or take?

How do we reward, recognise and support success?

- What does good look like?
- Who do we recognise, the individual or the team?
- What, in either or both, do we recognise?
- What does this say about what it takes to get on here?
- Who gets training, development and why? Is training oriented to help leaders manage down, challenge up or get the best out of each other?
- Is there training for the development of skills or culture, doing or being?
- How do we role model continuous improvement?

- How do we facilitate collaboration, communication and creativity?
- What space and time do we allocate for listening, reflection, review and fresh thinking?

Power, care and respect: three simple themes which inspire some hugely important questions. I hope some of them are useful for you to reflect on when you think of the organisation you are part of now.

Before undertaking this project, I did some research with senior leaders in the organisations I work alongside and cast out into my networks to seek the insight and perspective of their direct experience.

I wanted to test out a hypothesis around the 'say do' gap. What organisations say they value and what actually happens in practice which is a key indicator of alignment and trust.

I also wanted to evaluate practices specifically in terms of how they value coaching and feedback, which is a central foundation of successful Green and Teal organisations and is also present in highly successful Amber and Orange organisations, balancing out the power dynamics that can get in their way.

When I talk from here on in about coaching, I am not talking about qualifications, certification or the provision of services from an outside expert. I am talking about the day to day practices and the qualities of leaders who have mastered the art of open two-way communication. A conversation rather than a process and the kind of leadership that:

- Builds trusting relationships
- Facilitates greater collaboration, critical thinking, creativity, challenge and support
- Promotes fresh thinking, new behaviour, and outstanding results

Something that all leaders are capable of, provided that there is a clear commitment and purpose for doing so. And how this skill is used in organisations of all kinds to facilitate their on-going development and success.

My first question was:

How valued is coaching and feedback in your current organisation vs. previous organisations you have worked in? And why?

As you read some of the responses you may identify with some of the themes from your own organisation, or you may recognise some of the descriptions outlined in the previous chapter. I have outlined where I think these organisations sit in the Red to Teal spectrum. Maybe note down which ones stand out as particularly relevant or resonant for you right now.

It's not valued in the way it should be. There are examples of poor performance, fearful behaviour, doing what's going to get recognised rather than what's right everywhere you look, and the business suffers as a result. There is no emphasis at all placed on coaching or feedback as it feels like the people are not worth investing in. Staff turnover is high and the board don't seem to care. The HR Director almost takes pride in saying 'people self-select' here. I could never get my head around that. In previous roles/companies, people have been at the heart of the business and were less of a commodity. My old CEO once asked me

> how I'd got on with a project. I told him it was OK, but if I had the chance to do it again, I'd do a few things differently. 'That's ok,' he said, 'even if we shelve (the project), we spent that budget training you how to do it.' I was really taken aback by the difference between the two organisations: One is like the Wild West, it's emotive and personal. The second is more aware.

A great illustration of the energetic difference between leading as a coach (Green) vs. the hire and fire, unpredictability of Red.

> I think coaching and feedback is less valued in my current organisation than others I worked with previously. I think it's largely around culture and the self-awareness of senior leadership, particularly the CEO who sets the tone of the organisation. There is a sense that this type of development and way of working is fine for the subordinates and that the leaders

are already beyond the need for development. Feedback at the highest level is not welcome and receives defensive behaviour bordering on aggression. The middle layers react similarly to the way they see the senior people acting, so learned behaviour and the 'how to get along without rocking the boat' type of behaviours become prevalent. Those who have been exposed to coaching techniques and having been trained to provide feedback are receptive during learning and largely 'get it' however when out of the learning environment they mostly revert to type and resume previous behaviours. Where feedback is given, it tends to focus too much on perceived deficiencies rather than building on the positive.

Use of the words subordinates, lack of upward feedback and learned behaviour designed "to get along without rocking the boat" suggests Amber orientation.

The value placed on coaching is low, the focus is on cost and 'we know what we are doing'. But reality is we are walking on eggshells. People don't know how to give or receive feedback. Typically, the issues are about 'my area, my job, my team, my idea' etc when in fact it's all about 'our and together' when building the best approach. Being open means there might be another way, but their perceived failure of there being another way precludes people from discussing it. You don't always need to know the answer to the question. That I am still learning.

A leader wanting to drive more of a Green perspective within what is a competitive and individualistic (Orange) culture.

In the Big 4 accountancy firms, feedback was incredibly important – 360 feedback is the norm and every employee was expected to gather feedback throughout the year – not just at your annual appraisal! Every employee had a 'mentor'/Development manager in addition to their line manager. In part, this was to ensure you (as an employee) could discuss your developmental needs, how to move up the ranks and explore other opportunities to get involved in within the firm. You were encouraged to be involved in projects outside of your 'day' job to help develop you in other areas.

A highly developed achievement Orange culture, which fosters the same mindset of continuous improvement in its leaders.

I have been trained in hostage and crisis negotiation. The feedback sessions were constructive but also brutal. Every type of minor mistake or error was seized upon and dissected but with good reason – a negotiation using clumsy language, not listening effectively can have fatal consequences. This doesn't mean the objective was to crush the student (or qualified negotiator, as professional development was continual) but it was to develop individuals in a very pressurised environment to make sure they could deliver whilst under significant stress and potentially in isolation. Students new to negotiating were often stunned by the first few feedback sessions as the frankness was not seen in any other discipline. It is still the case that few areas focus so much on feedback. Outside of the above discipline I find few people prepared to have difficult conversations.

This last contribution I think really brings forth the importance of the quote at the beginning of this chapter. No one stage of development is better than another. Command and control have their place. When in an emergency situation, having a clear chain of command and structured way to respond where all individuals in a team know their role and the sequence of actions required undoubtedly makes success more likely. Order in chaos is all in the preparation and the backbone of all military and emergency service training, drills and ultimately high performance, when those they serve need them most. Being aware of the behaviour which best fits the context is key, and signalling really clearly when it needs to happen, and why, with a clear focus on what it takes to deliver high performance.

In short, command and control structures work very well in an emergency. But for leaders in such organisations, operating outside of an emergency response, how might other ways of communicating bring people with you? How can you liberate engagement, creativity and a willingness to step forward without simply mandating, creating a new policy or directive? And how can you apply feedback techniques with equal rigour when it comes to leadership behaviours as you do the development and refinement of technical skills or capability?

This is the essence of responsiveness, of not getting stuck in one model of leadership that is applied in all situations, to all people.

The 'say do' gap is where organisations can get themselves into trouble. When they try to don the clothes of one stage of development without being aware of what they need to take off or let go of to make it actually fit. In respect of the dimensions of power, care and respect:

- Empowering people is easy to say you want, a lot harder to achieve if those at the top are reluctant to give up control, of telling other people what to do, of coming up with solutions, and retaining a tight grip on an illusion that only they alone know what will happen in the future or are capable of determining what and how things should be implemented in response. Or indeed if the most senior stakeholders are reluctant to apply the same expectations of themselves that they do others. If feedback is important, no one can be above giving or receiving it.

- Values are pretty easy to create, and most companies have a variation of words which look pretty much the same even though their cultures and leaders do not. 'Innovation and teamwork are our life blood', 'we value your feedback' and 'learning and development are really important to us' are all platitudes you will see and hear in most corporate contexts. But what really matters are the attitudes and beliefs that underpin them, the codes of behaviour and day to day practices that bring them to life, as this is what gives a clue to what the organisation truly believes in and prioritises. What it truly cares about. Values when lived, provide a navigation system to fall back on, a source of guidance for behaviour—an inner compass. Especially when faced with a crisis, which is when old habits can emerge to puncture through the very best of intentions. Something that tends to be felt acutely by those in the wider organisation when any dysfunction in this regard is playing out at the very top.

- Mind-set really is everything. Over process, mandate, control and monitor anything and you will drive a mind-set of obligation, one where people go through the motions. Complying at best but doing so unwillingly, because they have been told they have to. Doing something because you genuinely recognise there is a benefit for you and others drives a very different energy, outcome and therefore sense of value (and ownership of that value).

So firstly, we must seek to look not at what the organisation says about itself, but what it does. If the two align, then great. Which includes, by the way, the organisations built on a Red paradigm. As long as everyone is clear about the rules of engagement and are happy to sign up to the reality of what that means then at least there is some kind of integrity, albeit one that usually comes at a cost to the individuals in those organisations. An environment driven by fear and the fight for survival will tend to drive some kind of compromise (in return for money or status). You do what you are told, turn a blind eye at times and do what you need to do to get by, rather than what might be—by any moral standard—viewed as right. These organisations rarely pretend that two-way dialogue matters and the senior execs who run them are usually well known for their aggressive outbursts which puts a stop to any kind of openness or honesty about anything they don't want to do or hear. And they are the least likely to ask for the opinions of others that may challenge their view or way of working. If that is the kind of organisation you find yourself in, then there really isn't much point talking about the concept of feedback. You make a choice to be in that kind of system and play by its rules, or you get out.

But for all other models, there is hope. That with sufficient role modelling, honesty and a clear purpose and focus on what great looks like, or could look like, greater self-awareness, growth and success is possible for the teams and employees who choose to work within them.

How to do that successfully is what we will explore.

Reflection Exercise 3

Complete the following exercise on the quality of the relationships you see with leaders around you (the team you are in, and/or those more senior)

Where are you now?

Which dimensions would you like to be different?

What part do you play in making that happen?

Use the scale below to indicate how each statement applies to your team. Be sure to evaluate the statements honestly and without over-thinking your answers

3 = Usually   2 = Sometimes   1 = Rarely

Statement	Score
I can say what I really think	
People really listen	
Issues are confronted openly	
Feedback happens daily, weekly (not just at annual reviews for example)	
Strengths & weaknesses are recognised and supported	
Help is given willingly and unconditionally	

Chapter 4: What great looks like

"Never doubt that a small group of thoughtful, committed, citizens can change the world. Indeed, it is the only thing that ever has."

Margaret Mead

Patrick Lencioni published a book, *5 Dysfunctions of a Team,* back in 2002 and remains a renowned consultant and thought leader. His book unfolds as a story of a fictional team struggling to compete in its marketplace but at the heart of it is a framework which is timeless in its insight and simplicity. There has not been one leader I have recommended to read this book who has failed to relate to the issues contained within it. If you know it the summary below will be familiar, if not see if you identify with any of the principles contained within the definitions.

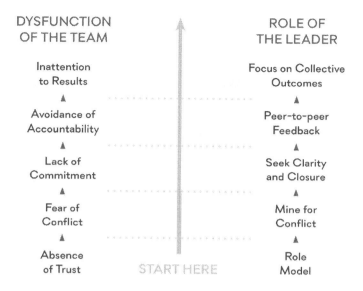

DYSFUNCTION OF THE TEAM	ROLE OF THE LEADER
Inattention to Results	Focus on Collective Outcomes
▲	▲
Avoidance of Accountability	Peer-to-peer Feedback
▲	▲
Lack of Commitment	Seek Clarity and Closure
▲	▲
Fear of Conflict	Mine for Conflict
▲	▲
Absence of Trust	Role Model

START HERE

Dysfunction 1: Lack of trust

The premise is that if you want results, however you define them, then trusting relationships is the foundation. This speaks to the ability of a group of people to trust the good intentions of everyone around the table, that they can trust that confidentiality can be respected where it is required, who can be open and honest with each other and let down their defences. Trust will not exist when team members are neither prepared to take the risk to be vulnerable and where they do not feel a level of psychological safety to be vulnerable (and you need both). When trust is absent, the underlying need will shift: to be right, to be strong and competent, to be protective and guarded for the fear that any vulnerability, truth telling, openness or exposed weakness will be exploited and used against them by their peers, or indeed, lead to some kind of reprisal from their boss. What you tend to observe in teams like this are defensive behaviours, pretence, reluctance to ask for help or provide assistance to others, a collection of individuals who are unable to leverage the power of the group and who instead spend their time rowing their own boats in their respective silos, at war with each other, but usually behind each other's backs.

Dysfunction 2: Fear of conflict

Healthy conflict flourishes when people feel free to talk about the issue at hand avoiding personal attacks, where there is a clear purpose to engage in meaningful dialogue in order to determine the very best solution for the team. Without a level of trust and integrity, conflict can't happen, and what it is replaced with is avoidance and artificial harmony.

To be clear, harmony is good but only if it comes from the ability to cycle through conflict and deal with the issues at hand. If you are in a team that cannot deal with conflict you tend to spend a lot of time 'offline' never making decisions that the group can commit to and avoiding the elephant in the room, in other words, speaking about the one thing that everyone knows—in fact is blindingly obvious to all—but all are too scared to say.

Dysfunction 3: Lack of commitment

Commitment is a function of *clarity* and *buy-in*. Teams who engage in healthy, productive conflict will more confidently be able to commit and buy-in to decisions. They make clear decisions, confident that they have the support from every team member. People tend to find it easier to buy in something when their opinions and thoughts on the matter are sought so a lack of commitment usually arises from not hearing all the teams concerns before making a decision, and no commitment is possible without debate. This comes back to previous points about use of power and is less about consensus decision making (which can result in watered down commitments that satisfy no one) –

but more holding onto the insight that people will more easily commit if their voices have at least been heard. That everyone around the table can get to the point where they can honestly say, '*I may not agree with your ideas, but I understand them and fully support them.*'

Dysfunction 4: Lack of accountability

If the team is to be accountable, everyone must have a clear understanding of what is expected of them, and to have bought into the same plan. Otherwise accountability is merely a concept which in practice is akin to nailing jelly to a wall. This dysfunction also speaks to the principle of each team member being accountable to the team and of not letting the team down when it comes to meeting follow-through of commitments, of working to high standards and the behaviours that drive them. In a high performing team, expectations are explicitly set so that it is the responsibility of each team member to hold one another accountable and to open and accept when others hold them accountable. In other words, high performing teams prize and practice peer to peer feedback, support and challenge and see it as, if not more, important as any feedback provided by the most senior person in the room. Fear of conflict and a lack of trust will hold teams back from holding each other to account, and so will any level of avoidance when it comes to reviewing and measuring their progress, on either 'the what' or 'the how'. So, it is crucial to make clear what the team's standards are, whether this is with regards to its output, its actions 'the doing', or its behaviours, 'the being'. Ambiguity on either is the enemy of accountability as it facilitates the group and the results they create, to go unchallenged.

Dysfunction 5: Inattention to results

A healthy team places team results as the most important goal. When all team members place the team's results first, the team will become results orientated. We not I.

'Our job is to make the results that we need to achieve so clear to everyone in this room that no one would even consider doing something purely to enhance his or her individual status or ego. Because that would diminish our ability to achieve our collective goals. We would all lose.'

When teams are not held accountable the team members tend to look out for their own interests, rather than the interests of the team. To overcome any inattention to results, leaders need to make the team's results clear for all to see, rewarding the behaviours that contribute to the results, not individuals who win at the expense of integrity, of others or to what matters to the organisation as a whole.

So, a different way of looking at success by looking at what so very often plays out in a team dynamic rather than through the lens of the system. This is an important one for any of you who may identify strongly with the cultural dynamics of the organisations described thus far but feel disconnected from any way of changing it. This is where to start, with what is in your sphere of control:

- how you show up to the leaders you work alongside
- how you lead your team
- how you lead yourself

My belief is that the core theme of how to communicate, collaborate, support, drive greater levels of creativity, challenge and critical thinking within any team dynamic align perfectly, no matter which organisational paradigm you belong to. If you are a leader that wants to live up to the promise that your organisation holds. If you do believe that taking the time to step back, think, be challenged, explore possibilities, speak up, learn from the experience and support others can stimulate and drive huge leaps forward in development, then coaching is likely to be something worth exploring.

If that is true for you, then at this point, the 3Ps are worth reflecting on:

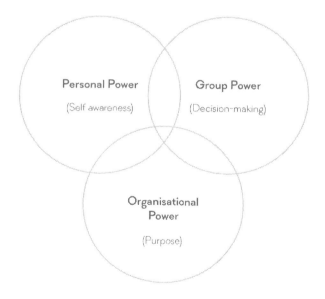

1) The Power of Purpose

First and foremost, what is it you really want? And why does that matter to you as an organisation, to your people, to your customers, to your stakeholders?

If you do buy into the notion that the ability to facilitate open and honest conversations that lead to clear decisions and accountability is a core leadership skill, one that many successful organisations embrace, what purpose do you want them to serve for you?

What do you want more of as a result?

- Challenge?
- Connection?
- Creativity?
- Honesty about issues?
- Critical thinking?
- Innovative solutions?
- Support?
- Confidence?
- Pace?
- Reflection?

- Openness?
- Listening?
- Collaboration?
- Empathy?
- Stretch for individuals?
- Trust?
- Self-awareness?
- Accountability?
- Action?

Purpose can exist at multiple levels: for leaders, for teams, for the organisation as a whole and is the only thing which will elevate any initiative, project, programme, plan or directive from becoming a tick box exercise. Something you do because HR have told you its mandatory, as part of a performance review process that is exercised once a year. Do anything because you have to do it, without really giving much thought to why and people will just go through the motions. Or you risk implementing a programme that teaches skills that do not serve the higher purpose for the organisation, or indeed address its limitations. Coaching, feedback and facilitation can drive all of the above. But some might be more important to you than others, either now or in the future.

2) Group Power and Decision Making

- Challenge?
- Who gets to decide?
- How do we decide?
- How do we as a group resolve disagreements and divisions in the event of us not being able to decide?
- And if we do not have a place at the decision-making table, what influence do we have as individuals or as a collective so that our voice is heard?

How to facilitate decision making in a group is the least talked about and most important of leadership skills, and requires a consciousness which, in my own experience, few leaders innately possess. Or as one insightful trainer once said to me, "Power is the one thing least talked about, especially by those who have it."

Power built on trust, rather than hierarchy, relates to the art of allowing people to open into a dialogue, to deepening understanding through the exchange of views and ultimately coming to a clear, concise and aligned view of the situation, the possibilities, the so what, and the next steps.

"We have boomerang subjects Nic," said one HR Director. "We talk about something, we can't agree. The conversation gets tense, the FD is someone who can't let stuff go, he's like a dog with a bone. Then people start to glaze over. At this point the Chief Exec makes a joke to lighten the mood but we don't resolve anything. The subject always comes back around at the next meeting and we do the same all over again."

If a pattern of not making decisions is one you are familiar with, then being conscious of your part in this is an important one. Are you generally the one with a view you share freely on most subjects, do you find yourself getting heated, frustrated or do you sit on the fence, go quiet, use humour to make light of discomfort, skip over debates, take them off line? Do you engage in conflict or avoid it? What, if anything, do you want to be different?

Facilitating the kind of open and honest dialogue that is a prerequisite for creativity, good decision-making and commitment is a role in itself. It is why senior teams often hire facilitators so that, for challenging or meaningful discussions, all parties can play an equal part in the dialogue. To move forward on the content of the discussion, whilst getting feedback and insight on how they have the discussion. This requires some trust, to let go of the facilitation process so that the group can focus fully on the outcome and what can be learned. Whilst the facilitator holds some power in respect of holding the group to their purpose and agreed behaviours, they let go of having any input into the decision. This is consciously agreed up front, failing to do so means that the person with the pen risks directing, leading the group to a decision that is based on their agenda. As a facilitator I may be asked for my insight, but whether the group wants to run with it is up to them.

Consciousness in respect of power requires a level of flexibility in the way power is exercised. How the group decides and who decides. I, we or you. In other words, where does it make sense for one person, the most senior in the room or the problem owner, to make the call? Where do you need the full unanimous buy in of all before proceeding and where can you delegate entirely and allow others to make the call? Which in itself implies a discipline not to meddle and change things if the call others make is one you don't like. There is power in letting go and allowing others the benefit of trial and error. And in doing so drives far greater levels of freedom, accountability, development and innovation than holding tightly to the reigns out of fear ever did.

3) **Personal Power and Presence**
- Who are you?
- What are the values and behaviours that matter most, no matter what?
- What is ok and not ok?
- Where is the line?
- And what happens if we cross it?

Gravitas is an energy, the kind you instinctively know when you are in the presence of it. It has a solidity, an intensity that commands trust and respect at very intuitive levels. When someone with gravitas speaks others generally want to listen, but speaking is often not necessary. You can feel it when they walk into a room. Do some people just have it? Yes, I think they do. Can it be learned? Yes, absolutely. Provided we want to develop, and are prepared to do the work, in three core areas:

Self-awareness

Know who you are and what you do brilliantly, then you are well placed to shine. This is your source of power. Alongside knowing what you aren't, having the humility to accept you will make mistakes, the realism to know you don't always have the solutions and the knowledge that when you surround yourself with talented and diverse individuals who really make you think differently, together you will always find a way. Balance, as in all else, is key. Building on strengths and addressing limits. For being clear on what our own limits and mistakes are will generally help others feel less inclined to cover up their own. Importantly, power is not to be confused with a drive for perfection or a desire to be seen as such. That is pretence. Flaky, insecure, easily shattered, an energy you can feel when in the presence of those prone to the fear of being found out. Gravitas has a different quality, one that is real, born of knowing oneself well, and being comfortable in that awareness.

Some of the most memorable coaching engagements for me have been working alongside people who have, up until that point, never looked at who they really are and who they have become. They have taken on other's criticisms, or indeed listened too astutely to their own, and either never fully realised the gifts they possess or had the courage to put themselves forward to be seen on a bigger stage. One client, a talented commercial director whose development I had the privilege to support in a couple of large organisations, was both surprised and delighted by the values strengths she uncovered in a 121-coaching session. "I should have been a judge," she said with a rueful smile. Having just explored the process to become a magistrate myself, I thought she had precisely the strengths, qualities, intellect and diverse experience they look for, should she want to. Turns out, that one conversation planted a seed. She went through the application process to become a magistrate and nailed it. She also rekindled her love of writing and published a book. It never ceases to amaze me what leaders are capable of when they finally see what others see, for themselves.

If this is an area which interests you, and you wish to explore it further, the tools and exercises outlined in Courage, dear heart will take you deeper.

Holding boundaries

This speaks to the ability to call out behaviours that are not in the interest of an individual, the group or the purpose of the organisation. "What you ignore, you condone," as a retiring Chief Exec said to me when I asked him on his greatest learnings from his 30-year career, 10 of which were at the very top of a very large organisation. A profound principle he had learned the hard way in dealing with challenging, unacceptable behaviours above and below him. His one regret being not having called out one of his direct reports sooner. Someone who drove the rest of the team beyond frustration to the point of stunned silence and disbelief for his propensity to talk with eloquence about concepts, stories and theory but not deliver, then play victim when challenged so that everyone felt sorry for him (and stopped challenging). He was a lovely man, whether he was aware of it or not, he was playing out a pattern that worked for him to a degree, until a new Chief Exec arrived, and it no longer did.

I observed the same thing working with another team and in a review the HR Director said, "You must have worked with some dysfunctional teams like this before Nic." "Actually, no. I have never come across a team quite as dysfunctional as this one," was my response.

Individually the team were lovely people, many of whom had worked together for many years. On the surface they all had long standing relationships. They were also very astute in their awareness of the issues they had as a team - a lack of trust, transparency, healthy conflict, feedback and alignment to a collective vision and goals. What they did have were individual goals aligned to their respective international silos and managers.

The problem was that in the absence of anyone holding them to account as a collective, the behaviours creating these outcomes had become ok: the moaning, withholding, defensiveness, silo working.

There is a principle when it comes to coaching, that without a clear gap you can't grow. You have to know you have a problem and want to do something about it. There has to be a motivation. And that motivation can come from a pull, a desire to be and do better. Or a push, a boundary held, a consequence of not doing so, a cost. The team didn't seem to have either.

They were miserable, for different reasons, but didn't appear to want to speak up and/or leave. Which sometimes shows up in cultures where people know that no one goes unless they are paid to. Instead leaders hang in, stuck in a holding pattern of negativity which they take out on each other. Meaning, that in some ways this particular team were right; the problem wasn't theirs. It lay with those more senior who were letting it happen. As it turned out, the person who most valued the alongside support was their line manager.

Holding boundaries means knowing what the limits are. For oneself as much as others. Those with strong sense of their own power know how to say no and mean it. To hold oneself and others to account when a behaviour is not serving us. To step up and say what needs to be said rather than circle endlessly in frustration, or avoidance. This aspect of power is entirely unrelated to rank, seniority or position. It is about mindset of responsibility, being crystal clear about what is ours to take on (and honouring that) and what is for others (and holding them to that).

Clarity which tends to have both an uplifting and trust enhancing impact for all concerned.

Role modelling

Role modelling is the commitment to practice what we ask of others. Anything less does not support base level integrity. Or inspire others to do the same. Akin to asking your kids to get off their phones, as you scroll emails on your phone. We have all done it, with not a leg to stand on.

I worked with one organisation, a global brand builder built on an Orange paradigm with a comprehensive set of HR practices and a commitment to talent, development, feedback and succession planning, which was practiced at all levels except, it would appear, at the very top. I remember talking to the CEO one day and I asked him directly why it was that he had failed to deal with underperformance in his board. "Because Nic I thought I could change them, that to accept they were not up to the job would be a failure on my part." I empathised with his desire to support his people. It is after all an admirable quality. But if, as leaders, we take total responsibility for the performance of others then the balance has tipped too far. He had made the underperformance about him, not seen the other as having a part to play. When we allow this to happen, and our own fear of failure is in the driving seat, there is usually a cost. In this case on his reputation, particularly amongst those more junior who were looking up wondering why certain individuals, many of whom went back a long way with him, were being allowed to get away with talking a good game.

A lapse on his commitment to practicing what he was preaching to others further down the organisation in relation to feedback and performance management had a consequence in the trust others had on his judgment. It also created suspicion about what it actually took to make it to the top. Was it merely a case of 'jobs for the boys'?

The truth of it was, he was highly competent and caring. Other leaders had a high level of respect for his intellect and insight, but he was someone who needed challenge to keep him being honest with those around him. I know when the day came to holding up the mirror to one particular individual, a detailed look over previous performance reviews revealed years and years of on target reviews which made landing the feedback that much harder for him when it became utterly unavoidable. Not to mention it being more of a shock for the director on the receiving end of that particular conversation.

If there is one thing senior executives need, it is people around them who are prepared to give them support and challenge. At work and at home. We can never climb too high for challenge, to accept help or to learn from our mistakes, and if anything is worth role modelling it is this.

If any of the themes so far have provoked some thought, about the organisation or the team you work within, for, or lead and there are elements you would want to improve or change, then the question becomes where can this start with you?

Reflection Exercise 4

Look back over this chapter at the headings above relating to Purpose, Group Power and Decision Making, and Personal Power. For each, write your thoughts to each question and any ideas that are already springing to mind:

Purpose: write down what you want more of for your team. 3 things max.

Group Power and Decision Making: think about a meeting, or process you want to sharpen? What is it you want to be different and why?

Personal Power: what are your own strengths and gaps? In which areas would you like to be stronger, more confident, more at ease?

Chapter 5: Holding up the mirror

"Do the best you can until you know better. Then when you know better, do better"

Maya Angelou

Before embarking on this book, I spent time developing a coaching programme with fellow coach and thinking partner Mark Pringle. As part of the creative process, we identified the attributes you tend to find in great leaders who coach, to which I have overlayed the energetic quality you often feel from their presence:

Creative thinking – the ability to stimulate ideas, invite new perspectives, come up with opportunities and possibilities, the spirit of continuous improvement. **Open, unbounded, free.**

Challenge – the ability to identify blocks, blind spots in thinking and behaviour, the willingness to look at what gets in the way of creativity, action, results. **Honest, purposeful, kind.**

Critical thinking – the ability to weigh up alternative solutions, look at issues and opportunities in balance, encourage and facilitate healthy debate with stakeholders before making a clear call. **Pragmatic, neutral, grounded.**

Collaborate – the ability to build strong, lasting, trusting relationships, to seek out talented people with diverse strengths, to want the best for, and with, others. **Proactive, respectful, generous**.

Communicate – the ability to lead open and honest two-way conversations, to listen without judgment and land the messages that count. **Engaging, clear, simple.**

Confidence – the ability to see the good in oneself and others, to offer support and belief where it is absent. **Strength, balance, care**.

The Mindset of Encouragement

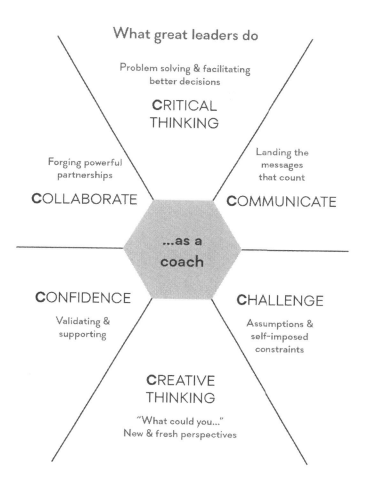

What great leaders do

Problem solving & facilitating
better decisions

CRITICAL
THINKING

Forging powerful
partnerships

COLLABORATE

Landing the
messages
that count

COMMUNICATE

...as a
coach

CONFIDENCE

Validating &
supporting

CHALLENGE

Assumptions &
self-imposed
constraints

CREATIVE
THINKING

"What could you..."
New & fresh perspectives

If the 6Cs makes sense to you in principle, the question then becomes can everyone become a coach?

What are the qualities required to be great at facilitating dialogue that lead to clear, committed action, either with individuals or in groups?

If you take a moment to cast your mind back over your career, who are the people who really stand out as successful leaders of people, who supported your own success? What qualities did, or do, you see and admire in them?

Here are a few responses to the latter question from clients, leaders I have worked with over the years. I have referenced the underlying attribute (based on the 6Cs) that I sense my clients are most drawn to.

What qualities do I admire in great leaders (who coach and give feedback)?

Challenge (mindset)

Their ability to provide empathy without sympathy, to not agree with 'poor me', that its not fair. They challenge and ask me how I can impact or influence the thing I am struggling with. If not, move on. They drive accountability, and hold me to account.

Creative thinking (shared experience)

They always listen first & intently – this encourages me to reveal even more! They ask really insightful questions that challenge my thinking, provide tasks to try between sessions which require me to feedback my success. The building of trust is key, also a credibility factor for respecting the views – have they been through it, have they crossed this bridge before, have they experienced team members needing this type of support. The best ones I have experienced bring their own vulnerability into the relationship – they are not superheroes. But they have experienced some of the challenges I have and have come out the other side.

Confidence (encouragement)

They were three people who I respected as leaders whose teams functioned well, who made me believe I could do things I didn't think were possible. One pushed me so far out of my comfort zone in a creative brain storming session one day, I admit I was very scared. But I remember that whole session to this day about thinking differently. By the end of that day I was buzzing and drawing!!! The other two both praised me for things I did naturally and highlighted that these were my strengths. It is very easy to focus on what you are not so good at, we don't naturally see our abilities the way others do.

Creative thinking (learning partner, spark)

They keep the pace on, don't tell, but guide with a toolbox that has so many compartments that help to talk through a situation, the goal, how and what if.... They don't let me hide, they listen, question, cajole and laugh with me.

Collaboration (thinking partnership)

The ability to communicate and engage, to put people at ease v quickly. I feel like I have known them a long time, we are engaging rather than listening, it's an on going positive, two way conversation where I don't feel like the dunce, we are truly problem solving.

Critical thinking (sense making, depth)

The way they always make the subject we're addressing 'bigger and rounder' and turn it into something you can address and do something with i.e. when we start talking about an issue they help isolate it, separate it and highlight how it's the same as something else. I admire their way to connect what we're talking about to what really means to me and put it in a personal context of my goals, my way of thinking and my motivators. I also admire how their knowledge and expertise is not their armour. First and foremost, they are a person, personable and so human. It's not until you get into what you're doing that their skills come to the fore.

Collaboration (leveraging strengths)

I think the thing I most admire (in a previous line manager) is that she role models exactly the right behaviours, she challenges where appropriate, moves with pace where possible and brings people with her (identifying very quickly who will help and who will hinder and then managing them out). She keeps the bigger picture in mind all the time so you know you can move with her with confidence. She listens intently, makes the time for people and then reflects on everything you say. I particularly admire her ability to do that in the moment (I often need a day to come back!). We could have great debates where I bring a theory, she picks it apart, it gets a bit frustrating but then an hour later we are both in a much better place! But she has a way of doing that which makes you feel like you were really part of it, your contribution has been made and then improved upon.

Confidence (support out of comfort zone)

They helped me to create a strategy, a vision for the future, to make a difference within the business. I focus very much on the detail, getting stuff done, creating a cohesive team. I can find hundreds of other things to do before I create time for this important work, as I find it difficult to do, so I also need someone to hold me accountable, to ask good questions to ensure I don't just revert back to what is comfortable.

Challenge (hiding, prevarication)

What I most value is the way they challenge my thinking. The interaction promotes increased self-examination that is often not the case when reflecting on my own performance in the preceding weeks or months. The way of chasing down every issue so that there is no hiding place or chance to prevaricate is also very helpful and it's done in a non-threatening way whilst being very thorough. For me it is the 'holding up the mirror' techniques that are most powerful.

Confidence (to be real)

What I admired most in my last boss was her approachability. She was fun, real, professional. She also was not scared to show emotion. I have worked in so many organisations where men don't, and been told that if your are emotional you are not being a good leader. She taught me that people can perform and be serious professionals without being so stuffy. Millennials are looking for that. She also had the time of day for anyone, had your back and gave very clear honest feedback. She was also honest about when she was having a moment, which gave me the permission not to be perfect.

Communication (with a mentor and equal)

Credibility for me is the ability to create strong first impression, be an effective communicator and active listener. Have clear pedigree, experience, 'scars' and demonstrate clear values. Credible individuals are able to influence others inside and outside their organisations. Those who can't influence can achieve very little.

There are a few common themes which come through from this lived experience of what works for the receiver. If the 6Cs show us what great leaders who coach do, I think this feedback shows us how:

- *Questions to challenge thinking*
- *Listens to build trust and rapport*
- *Valued for their expertise, learning, experience, presence, behaviours, ability to influence*
- *Encourages the positive*
- *Consistently direct and honest*

There is a foundation of supportiveness (they see and genuinely want the best for us) which opens us up in two ways–to hear whatever needs to be said and to make us think. I surrounded myself with people who will tell me when I am not showing up at my best or how I can improve. When I'm heated, frustrated, in my head, doing too much, then it becomes all the more important that those who love me will go out of their way to tell me straight. Who have the guts to tell me something I may already know but, for whatever reason, have lost sight of. The teachers, colleagues and creative partners I seek out are those I admire, who willingly share their own experience and come at things from a very different angle to me. For it is in thinking for ourselves, with a little prompting and fresh stimulus, which provides those moments where our eyes shine with realisation of an approach we had not previously considered. And when these approaches work, it makes me want to go back for, and give back more, to those in my network.

When I ask leaders what they most want help with, the list is always strikingly similar across the many coaching engagements I do, and was also consistent across the research I did for this book:

- *Saying what I really think, including saying no, especially upwards*
- *Confidence to challenge attitude and behaviour (and being clear enough for feedback to register)*
- *Building trust, overcoming the avoidance of conflict*
- *Understanding and utilising our strengths (and shoring up each other's weaknesses) so that we are better together*
- *How we make coaching and feedback part of our conversations, a part of how we are, not just at 121s and appraisals. That we proactively ask for it – how am I doing?*

What they really want is more confidence, more recognition and more day to day practice having the conversations that matter. They want to learn. Influence more powerfully. Build trust.

Interestingly when it comes to learning from past mistakes, it was often what people failed to say that they reflect on most, rather than what was said clumsily, with good intent. Revealing that what we most wish to receive is perhaps what we most need to think about giving to others.

What feedback do you most regret not saying?

Probably failing to provide objective feedback to my previous CEO when he most didn't want to hear any. Of all the Directors in the business, I was probably best trained and in the right space to have been more forthright in providing feedback however felt that it would have been a waste of time and may have created a fuss for no positive outcome. Maybe if I'm honest there's a bit of avoidance there on the grounds of having a quiet life.

I look back at a situation when I moved to a new role & location where a member of the team had decided to move into the Managers office prior to me joining. I left the situation as was rather than tackling it on day 1 which then meant that I had continual difficulties trying to manage that individual as the ongoing feedback and relationship was soured on both sides.

I think the feedback I most regret not giving sooner and owning sooner was with my ex-husband. I was a lot younger in my first marriage and was very worried about the perceptions and judgements of others and of my own fear of failure. If I had given the feedback sooner, it would have saved a lot of time and heartache for all.

I regret not giving a peer feedback about a number of things in the way he operated alongside me, making my role more difficult. I was avoiding conflict but ultimately it made my situation untenable. I regret that because that person would have dealt well with the feedback, which was that they should work better as a team and less as a lone ship, trying to solve everything alone.

Telling my work colleagues that I knew what they thought of me although they pretended to be supportive when they did not actually mean it. I would like to be more direct with my feedback as I have a tendency of not wanting to be seen as a 'bad' person. I need more confidence in tacking issues head on rather than a softly approach whilst preserving the need not to upset others.

I didn't tackle an issue with an individual, instead thinking I could support them to be better. I couldn't and didn't, they just weren't up to the job and I didn't deal with it.

For me to speak out/stand up and be counted more in the organisation and I just don't do it. One previous line manager described me as the secret rebellion – 'you have got all your rebel clothes on and guns fired up ready to shoot then you just didn't take them to the frontline.' Ouch. This is quite hard to write as it's so true. I think I'm trying to do it but I often fall at the first hurdle and instead of carrying on I just shuffle off to the side.

When somebody does something that upsets or annoys me and I don't deal with it and tell them at the time. I have lots of instances where I have bitten my tongue, the opportunity to deal with it has passed and I have subsequently carried it around with me, mulling it over in my mind, which in turn has made me unhappy.

I'm a massive reflector so there is a lot of stuff I have in my head that I wish I had said. Not providing my previous line manager with the right feedback to get him engaged, to build the relationship, to be honest. Not doing that meant it was a false relationship, which is a shame.

I wish I had felt more empowered to give feedback to senior leaders. This actually had nothing to do with them and everything to do with me.

Again, probably with my bosses, not giving feedback on the extreme workload and the fact I was unable to cope. I coped – but at the risk of a burnout – and that's not healthy in the long run. I was also working all the extra hours to protect my team from having to do the same.

It would be the more positive stuff on a more regular basis. I am naturally a person who critiques quickly and whilst this can be good in some circumstances it means that I see what I perceive as flaws very quickly. This ends up being my focus.

Giving feedback to a former employee. I think she lacked self-awareness in some instances and she personally would have benefitted from hearing some of it but once she had decided to leave, I wasn't sure it was my battle to have.

Saying no more. I was always trying to be 'liked' which meant a lot of time and effort from my side but not much reward. I was told that I was spreading myself too thinly and therefore not keeping the people that mattered happy – including the most important people in my personal life too!

I hope you have seen in the above something that also resonates for you. A reminder perhaps that we are all very similar and that seniority does not preclude us from having fears.

Fears about what people will think of us is we were to say what we really thought.

Fears about what the outcome might be for the relationship if issues are put on the table to be worked through rather than skirted around and ignored.

Fears about our own ability to deal with and confront people who are 'challenging' or who, maybe more accurately, are merely different to us in some way?

People who are very rational or emotional can be equally difficult depending on what end of the spectrum we ourselves lie. "If I say what I think they will cry and I don't know how to handle that," is something I often hear and, without wishing to generalise here, mostly from men. Expression of emotion in any form is what it is, a release, which passes. Release is usually a good thing. It allows us to move forward. Suppression of emotion is what can get us into trouble. Anger can turn into resentment, fear to withholding, denial to apathy and avoidance.

Bad experiences over time can certainly colour the lens that we apply to all relationships and people we come into contact with. As one MD I work alongside put it:

"I feel a lot of my team are 'damaged' from previous experiences of working in different cultures, so you have to spend a lot of time undoing the learned behaviour. It takes a good 12 months for a new team member to trust us enough to accept the feedback and begin to flourish. I also see some team members struggle to give feedback to peers, they use humour or sarcasm which is often misunderstood. We always try to encourage team members to think about how they would want to be treated if the tables were turned – i.e. Would they want to know? How would they like to be told?"

So, for me there is an important insight here about embodying as leaders what we want to see from others. If someone doesn't listen, then listen. Listening fully, wholeheartedly, earns the right to then be heard. Treating others as we would want them to treat us. If we were doing something that had a fundamental detrimental impact on others, most of us would say we would want to know. So why would we treat others any differently? Standing on solid principles or values like this are more likely to give us the courage to deal with any situation, regardless of whether we have encountered it before or not.

And what happens when we challenge those fears head on, how many of them are in fact imagined?

I received one email from an HR Business Partner who has been both a former colleague and client.

"I'm involved in an important piece of work at the moment and a senior leader asked for something today. On a call they asked a question that wasn't fully answered. I could sense it was important for them, so I gave them a call and gave some feedback, acknowledging what they were doing. They could not see or hear the positive impact they were making because no one was telling them. I

said, 'You are a great leader you are showing us the way, sharing those realistic views and holding us to account.' I could sense the relief. I was able to shine a light on the reality, to say what others may have been reluctant to say, and it made a difference. The key lesson: it doesn't matter what your status is, just listening shining the light on the things that matter can give someone the energy to carry on. I'm glad I took the path less travelled; I know that person needed the time to stop, listen and reflect. And a trusted relationship can endure anything!"

And that really goes to the heart of it. Building relationships that can support openness, honesty, challenge, feedback, commitment to action and ultimately outstanding results, are built on trust. The more trust we have, the more likely we are to take a risk. In saying what needs to be said, whether that be to acknowledge what is great in someone or to challenge them. Depending on your mindset, both can be surprisingly hard. The more trust we have, the more willing we will be to open to inviting feedback, to ask the question, "How am I doing?" Perhaps even more important for those at the top if you genuinely want no one to be above receiving it.

Reflection Exercise 5

Who are the great leaders you have worked with over the years?

What qualities have you admired in them? Did they ever know? (If you never told them it really isn't too late!)

Using the 6Cs as a reference and/or the exercise you did at the end of chapter 3, what do your peers and team would think, feel and say about you?

(More resources on seeking quality feedback against the 6Cs either via 360 or face to face are to be found at the end of this book).

Chapter 6: Leadership mindsets and practices

"The stronger the why, the easier the how becomes"

Jim Rohn

If feedback is something you want to get sharper at, then we need to go back to the essential elements of relational connection or indeed disconnection outlined earlier (Chapter 3) from which trust centres.

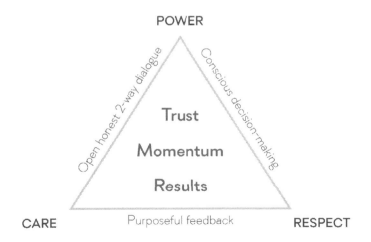

And in the context of seeking to get the best out of others and indeed oneself, no matter what the situation, then it is these three elements that require some preparation (mindset) and practice (skills).

Power and Control

The first is learning what you can control and what you cannot.

In spite of what we might think (or at times wish for) we have little control over anything other than ourselves. We are free to choose what we do, say, how we show up. Which provides us with one upside: total freedom, and one downside: total responsibility. An alluring sought after but double-edged sword, by which I mean when we understand we have total control over our own attitude and behaviour it is immensely liberating. True accountability always is. But truly owning and embodying this power comes with a responsibility that also requires us to give up blaming events or other people for why we do what we do. Or not do.

It requires us to look within rather than what is out there.

"For me, one's inner power comes from knowing the self, deeply and clearly. I'm getting to that place of understanding when I am angry, who or what part of me is not feeling fulfilled and missing a key. I don't always search nor research the self in these times, but I do recognise when I've lost my power.

As well I understand that we each hold and know power differently, where one might feel a sense of pressure and express it through movement, lashing out, screaming or isolating themselves, another may feel it through expression and so drama would come up or the want to create drama which is really to throw a ball somewhere else so it won't get dealt with." Atarangi Muru, Maori teacher, leader and healer.

I have been working with Ata now for a couple of years, learning and training in Maori healing arts and practices. What she is speaking to is self-awareness: knowing when we feel that deep sense of calm, connection and clarity. Clocking the times we don't (quickly) and being aware what impact this has on our relationships with others and the results we create. Catching ourselves when repeat dramas play out, or in other words getting to know the games we can play to take control of a situation through others:

- Do we get defensive, frustrated, angry, aggressive, blunt, rude and abrupt?
- Do we indulge in poor me stories, and give in to moaning, whining and excuses, either our own or of others?
- Do we chase others, micro-manage, find ourselves picking over details, quick to criticise what others do and say?
- Do we withhold information, make ourselves unavailable, get cagey, vague? Do we shut down, withdraw, make others pay by cutting them out?

These control dramas: The Intimidator, the Victim, the Interrogator and the Aloof are described by James Redfield in his book The Celestine Prophecy. Some dramas headlined above you may instantly relate to. We all have our fall backs to some degree or other. Some may irritate you intensely when you encounter them in others. The Intimidator and Interrogator are the most openly aggressive, whereas the Aloof and the Victim seek to draw others in and gain attention in more passive ways. What is interesting is that energetically, opposite dramas tend to attract. Intimidator and Victim, Interrogator and Aloof.

Intimidator	Aloof
• Takes energy by threat • Forces people to pay attention using fear	• Gets energy by acting coy and 'hard to get' • Often acts clueless • Tells redundant stories even if you've heard them
Interrogator	Poor Me
• Steals energy by judging and questioning others • Makes others feel inferior by finding faults in others	• Takes energy by making others feel guilty • Complains about problems and rarely states solutions

All of them are in some way an avoidance of responsibility, but we play them out because they give us an illusion of control, of getting what we want from others through manipulation. Which we keep doing for as long as these games work. Until of course they don't, and we come up against someone who calls it out and refuses to play along.

True power (rather than manipulation) is rooted in self-awareness. The ability to master one's own attitude, no matter what the situation. If you are interested in looking at this more deeply for yourself, *Courage, dear heart* outlines the practical tools, frameworks and steps to understanding and managing our mindset, and therefore our behaviour, or state.

What I would say is that the purpose for looking deeper at mindset is important. For me, it is so that we do better. That with greater awareness and determination, we can help ensure that the predictions, assumptions and (over) generalisations our minds create about the future and the demands and judgments we make of ourselves and others can be understood, overcome and an entirely new set of outcomes created. And in doing so, that we become more of who we really are, at heart. The purpose of examining our mindset is not to master a process. It is not to go around in circles, analysing ourselves and past events to death. This can have the unintended consequence of merely reinforcing our fears and the pathways in our brain that harden and narrow our responses. Where we simply remain stuck in our story, with an eloquently expressed rationale for why we are stuck.

When it comes to mindset, if you wish to go deeper do so with a commitment to move forward. If you go into it to master a process, to analyse and keep analysing, you may find yourself very aware of the theory but still going around in circles.

The real art of managing our mindset is in the practice. In the gritty reality of making things real, in the now. Feeling that sense of calm, connection and ease in splendid isolation with no distractions is relatively easy. Like going on holiday, which is beautiful for a short time. But we come back to reality eventually, and one or two days back at work is usually enough for us to forget we even had one. As it is only when we work alongside other people we can start to come up against limits. They don't do what we want, when we might want it, or they have traits that annoy us. And if that was not frustrating enough, the truth is we have no control over any of it. We cannot 'make them' do or be anything at all.

Realising the power we hold, and that which we do not, can be both frustrating and a relief depending on our perspective. Frustrating if we resist and refuse to let go of control. Relief when we do.

Understanding our power allows us to stop taking everything that other people do so personally. It can also unhook us from trying to fix or protect other people from the truth and reality. When viewed through a lens of facilitating and encouraging responsibility—supporting the self and others to step up—protection becomes a rather pointless endeavour. And so is playing victim, hiding behind all the reasons why we can't be honest or do something about the thing we keep moaning about because of what someone may or may not do in retaliation. If you read the regrets my clients had about feedback not given, most allude to a loss of power. Which had everything to do with them and not the individual they regretted not being honest with.

But if you do see that a pattern is repeating, where there is some kind of push and pull dynamic happening in a relationship, where you feel your energy drained by the undercurrent of something important unsaid then it is likely a drama is playing out. Which will continue until we decide to draw a line and not play out the game any longer. All it requires is a shift in mindset. Seeing patterns with fresh perspective, and making a choice from a very solid, grounded state (as opposed to one driven by fear).

One client wrote to me after our coaching engagement:

"I'm in my last 2 weeks of work and I can honestly say that I have zero regrets whatsoever (about leaving). Nothing is changing but I've been practicing the 'new' real me out in meetings and I've had a few comments which is really helping with my confidence. A couple of operators have said to me, "I can't believe you are leaving, it's taken me until now to realise that we really need to listen to you!" - could be a back handed compliment, but I'm putting it down to my new 'straight talking but delivered with empathy and humour' self."

Made me smile. It is funny how once a decision is made, like this one to leave, we feel able to let go. And once free to be more ourselves, power is restored, something that others immediately pick up on.

This rebalancing of power (in ourselves) drives something we do have in relation to others – the power of influence. Which includes presenting others with the choice, to step in, step up or to step out.

I coached one senior exec and an MD struggling with a relationship issue who reflected on their own change of mindset when it came to power:

"The insight that you can't change other people so you need to change your attitude towards them and own the problem made a huge difference for me, as I had spent a lot of wasted time and years moaning about others and it was making me bitter. Realising it was up to me to own that problem and change my attitude towards people has made me much more decisive and action orientated."

"I felt under pressure from my manager who I thought had no technical knowledge of the role or awareness of the actual job and who had admitted to 'force ranking' me as underperforming as part of an HR process, where he said one of his team 'had' to be below target. You asked me, "How does this make you feel? Do you feel that you could achieve better if you had a different Leader? If that leadership isn't likely to change then it is your choice

to stay and continue to feel this way, or you could go somewhere else and be valued and recognised." I was allowed the time to go through emotions and express my thoughts and feelings which then gave me confidence. I found a new role and left and am still in that new business having been promoted 3 times."

When we own what we can control, our own mind-set, behaviour and choices, things tend to get a whole lot easier. Whether it is you as a leader in the position of developing those around you or thinking about the development of your own career.

We have the power to choose our own attitude and behaviour in any circumstance. We can choose how we want to be, and it is entirely down to us. It is no one else's fault. Neither is it the fault of the situation we are in. And if true accountability is something we want more of in our teams and organisations, then our primary job is to lead ourselves more powerfully. Which for any leader wanting to influence, engage, and develop others in pursuit of a meaningful collective purpose then this is a principle worth holding dear to one's heart. As any interaction with others will tend to generate a better outcome if you are communicating from your best self, which we tend to operate from when we consciously choose how we want to be rather than acting out, reactively, from our worst.

What this power also allows is an assurance that if there is something you want to say to another, you cannot control what they do with the information. At best you may influence their actions or behaviour. Ultimately, we all have a choice. To stay, grow, create, engage, support. Or not. So, for anyone managing attitude issues or if you know you have checked out yourself, this is the area to take a closer look at. And what choices you have that you may not be acknowledging.

"I had coaching which included 360. My peers fed back that I would come across as blunt, disenageged and argumentative. I was always thinking that it was the other person's fault, but truth was I had quite a part of play in a situation happening. It gave me the realisation that the way you act, your demeanor, could unravel all that great delivery in a heart beat. The challenge I got also helped me to remember there was a 4th choice. A reminder that there is always another an option that

you are not considering. This opened my brain up, I was not backed into a corner as much as I thought. It was massively liberating."

"What I learned from coaching with you was the power of choice. I had a situation where one of my team came to me to complain that he just didn't get on with his line manager. I told him that I want to support both of them, that I would coach him and hire a mediator if needed, but I was not going to fire either of them, and that they would need to learn how to get along. What I also did say was that he would have to choose if that was a journey he wanted to go on. I gave him some time to come back to me. He decided he wanted to leave but sent me the most beautiful note thanking me. All I really did was give him my full support whilst being very clear that I was not going to fix the problem for him or tell him to suck it up. The power was his to choose."

"Nic you taught me about what was in my power to influence and what was not. Now I think can I influence it yes or no, and if not, I let it go. I am more effective, and I stress less."

And that is what tends to come with a conscious use of power, a win-win.

Care and Closeness

This is an important one when preparing for what leaders often call 'difficult conversations'. Difficult only because one party doesn't want to say whatever needs to be said, because they fear that the other won't want to hear it, and the fallout would be too much (an accusation, an ending).

I know one coach colleague of mine who detests the label. But I am not sure that rebranding them courageous conversations helps. Not unless we have faced into why they are difficult for us and choose care, over fear. Care in terms of both purpose, and compassion.

It is true that if we go into anything thinking, or more accurately fearing, it is going to be difficult then it probably will be. The mind is a powerful generator. It drives predictions, judgments and conclusions about pretty much everyone and everything we encounter that rattle around as an endless dialogue in our own heads. With our most severe criticism saved for ourselves. Often if left unchecked, these predictions will be grossly inflated, built up in our minds as much bigger than often is the case when reality is faced. What is also true is that if we go into something fearing the worst, we tend to tighten up in some way that makes the very thing we fear most even more likely to happen.

Take for example giving feedback on behaviours that are in some way holding you, the team or the organisation back. I help leaders give feedback for a living, so it is pretty standard for group or individual coaching to include me being on the receiving end of an extensive list of moans and gripes about what others are or are not doing. Have you told them? Is always my next question, closely followed by why not? Which then allows for all the excuses to come out. Or a pause whilst they reflect on why in truth they haven't, followed by a sheepish look.

If there is a strong purpose for you, for the other person, for the performance of the team then chances are this is a conversation that needs to be had. If there isn't a clear purpose then, as a leader, you have a choice to let it go. And by that, I mean really let it go, in other words not spending any more airtime in your head or in the company of others moaning about it.

This is where care and closeness really come into play. If there is a purpose, you know why it is important to raise an issue, put forward an idea, or ask a question that no one else seems to be asking. If you care about why doing any of these matters to the success of the team and the organisation, its stakeholders, customers or consumers, then you will say it. And saying it often is precisely what clears the air, creates a space for new thinking, new solutions and brings people and teams closer in the process.

As one HRD said to me, *"I gave a board member feedback about his lack of congruence between his communicated values, his actions and the impact this had on me. It was hard because I wanted to be honest and true to my own experience and I really wanted to keep the relationship and to stay and progress in the organisation. Actually, in giving the feedback it completely saved the relationship and rebuilt respect between us, it also made him start to consider his congruence and impact. This relationship is one of my strongest relationships now, many years on."*

Trust is built through cycling through conflict. The trick is to be clear why you are saying what you want to say. If there is an honourable purpose, in other words, genuinely for the benefit of the individual and team, and feedback is given with that level of thought and intention I think it's possible to say anything. If there is not a clear purpose, and a question or comment is expressed with traces of anger, sarcasm, judgment, finger pointing and blame, people will intuitively feel the energy being expressed rather than the words themselves. This is what creates disconnect, when care is not present. When communication is masked with humour, when it is in fact an attack, or an offloading of all that is 'wrong' with the other person from a place of perceived superiority. When we communicate without humility or heart, when it is designed more to cover our own back rather than be genuinely for the benefit of the other person receiving it. When we present a performance framework to someone with hoops they need to jump through when we know deep down that they have already reached their level, are struggling emotionally and are out of their depth. That is when disconnect becomes almost inevitable, and we can end up in a worse position with the issue remaining unaddressed and a chasm in the level of trust between both parties.

So always take care. Which sometimes means not giving feedback in the moment if you are not in the space to embody the requisite care, fully.

A lack of care will leak. People will feel judgment, blame, contempt, or the flatness of obligation where you are leading them through a process to tick a box however skilled you think you may be at hiding it. Care or the absence of it will work like a mirror either way, making it more likely that we get back whichever we choose to put out.

Respect and recognition

Whilst power and care relate to mindset, there are four specific skills I would highlight for consideration in the context of building trusting relationships.

1) Recognising strengths

If you are someone who knows they are very good at spotting inconsistencies, issues, weaknesses, what has not been done—which is after all, a great strength—then it can require practice to ensure that communication is delivered with balance. The unintended consequence of not paying attention to this one is that others can buckle under the weight of constant criticism, even if that is not what is intended. I have in the past worked for someone like that, I also work alongside senior teams who work for MDs who are like this. Their drive for constant improvement (or one might even say perfection) can drive them relentlessly to laser in on what could be better rather than recognising what is already great. And whilst the fear of never being enough, and/or the desire to always look at what can be fixed and improved might be what drives them personally, it may not be what drives and motivates everyone else around them. And this is another aspect of leadership where it pays not to make it all about us. The way we are wired is not the only way, or indeed the best way. We are all different. Recognising the need others have for reward, praise or recognition of strengths they may not even see themselves is important: to build confidence and inspire even greater levels of motivation to tackle the rest of the mountain to be climbed. Now I am not talking about false positives, trotting out some platitudes before you hammer people with a list of stuff that has not been done. But a practice of taking time to seek out balance, to acknowledge the behaviours and people who genuinely deserve recognition in spite of whatever challenges might exist.

The other aspect of balance to consider is how successful might we all be if we were encouraged to step into roles that played to our strengths rather than develop areas of weakness. As we saw in chapter 2, Teal organisations often look at talent through the lens of what skills, expertise, experience and qualities they bring that are going to get the best results, not what individuals need to be to fit a set structure and role. They prize the sole contributors and functional specialists and find ways to reward and recognise this that are uncoupled from hierarchy. In other words, there is no prerequisite to lead people in order to progress upwards, an assumption which is the norm for Orange and Amber organisations in light of their fixed hierarchical structures, even if basic levels of empathy and relationship building are not present. There would also be no expectation that a senior HR professional take a development position as a Marketing Director to prove they have commercial acumen, which I have witnessed. Unsurprisingly maybe, this particular well-intentioned endeavour ended in disappointment for all concerned. Whilst our awareness of our deficiencies is, in itself, a great asset, it does not always mean we can fundamentally eradicate them. We can round their edges, at best. Neither does this mean that development purely focused on fixing weaknesses should be encouraged, especially if in doing so it means that our strengths cannot shine.

As one senior exec said to me during the research phase for this book:

"I would love to help people do more of what they are good at and enjoy, and less of what they are not good at and don't enjoy. In companies, like in schools, we have templated ways of doing things and templated expectations (role profiles, performance management) but I really do think we can approach things more flexibly. What if we could match up people's aptitude, creativity, skills and ideas with directions the business needs to go in order to innovate and drive growth and change? We might end up with more cross functional teams

but surely a happier, more fulfilled and dynamic workforce."

A true expression of Teal thinking if ever there was one.

2) Listening

The second important aspect of trust building, I think, is the ability to listen, and to be present when listening. This is an art and is worthy of running a training course all of its own given its importance, and how many different types of listening there are in practice.

Firstly, we have **non-listening**, when you are physically present but not listening at all. There in body but not in spirit, which usually involves listening whilst multi-tasking, looking at your phone, writing an email, being in a meeting whilst simultaneously surfing online or sending a text message. This can also involve looking at the person, nodding occasionally and saying yes, whilst the mind is somewhere else entirely. Either in the future thinking about your next meeting or item on the to do list, or where you are mulling over something that has happened in the past that you are unable to let go of. Most meetings would be considerably more productive if various devices and others means of receiving communication were removed. This forces people to become more present and aware of who, in that moment, is actually a priority.

Selective listening is where you are focused on picking out the bits you want to hear, that builds an argument or picture that you already have in your mind. This is the classic listening technique that can happen in meetings, where one aspect of what someone says is used to put another entirely different point on the table. Giving the illusion of alignment but where, in reality, two or more people are actually talking at entirely cross-purposes. As a facilitator I often find myself picking this up. In a board meeting recently the chief exec and another director were in a dialogue, one said they were in agreement and said something completely different with a face that had disagreement written all over it. I called this out, "You don't look like you agree," which prompted a far more honest contribution and an admission that whilst he said yes, he really meant no. There is not much to be gained from artificial harmony or the endless circling that often happens in meetings, the long speeches where individuals talk at each other with the rest switching off in the process. If you have ever left one meeting to find your peers disagree with what was actually agreed, then you can be sure selective listening is the root cause. Selective listening is also a classic failure of performance reviews where an individual goes away only remembering what they perceive to be negative comments or feedback rather than any of what was acknowledged as positive. As human beings we can be masters of picking up on anything which confirms our own deeply held views, whether this be positive or negative. We love to prove ourselves right. To check for selective listening, ask the other person what they have heard and you will soon see if they are oriented to an agenda, or only taking in one aspect of what is being said. This is particularly important when communicating with those who lack confidence or self-esteem, where truly hearing balance and taking in the positive is even more important.

Reflective listening is more present. This is where the individual is listening with a purpose to re-express what is being said by the individual or a group. Playing back what the other is saying so that it can be easily condensed, re-framed. This can be effective in helping others to get clear what they really mean and find a form of words that summarises their current state, dissatisfaction or want. Importantly there is no agenda to do anything with what is being said, merely to interpret or translate. This is often used in qualitative consumer research, listening exercises with employees about what is working and what is not, and in mentoring where the purpose is to help another get clear but importantly not attempt to fix, change their perception or control the outcome. Reflective listening remains unattached. You listen for the benefit of the other person, not you.

Active listening has an action-oriented agenda. Where you are listening to respond or reply to what the other is saying. This is an important one for creative, decision-making and alignment sessions where there does need to be dialogue that leads to a clear outcome, an idea, a 'so what?' The active part is important where the full engagement, input and presence of all those around the table is required to make the very best decision and ensure all conditions, assumptions, options and perspectives are made explicit to support that decision. The other really important foundation for active listening is response, which is very different to react. Reaction will often arise in the form of defensiveness, any attempt to prove the other person wrong, shut them down, or descent into judgment and blame. Reaction is infectious in that it tends to invite the same in others around the table and will close down an open and honest exchange of ideas, dialogue and debate. Responsiveness requires a purpose to work through whatever is being said, to remain open, to allow what needs to come up and trust that this will support the individual and the team to get to a better place.

Empathic listening goes a little deeper and is where the sole purpose of listening is to understand. This is an important step on from active listening, beyond merely the words that are being said. Empathic listening is inherently more intuitive and seeks to read the body language, the unconscious signals we all give away when we communicate. The reality is as human beings we are masters of empathy whether we recognise this in ourselves or not. Research by psychologists (Prof. Albert Mehrabian – University of California in Los Angeles) back in the 60s found that 7% of communication registered comes from the words we say, 35% comes through tone, the remainder from what the body gives away involuntarily. When we do consciously seek to listen with empathy and really see people fully as we listen, it is possible to pick up on the underlying meaning of what is being said and indeed, what is not being said. Using our intuition in this way is the key to unlocking truly great feedback. Listen fully, wholeheartedly and you will pick up on the nuances that others give away all the time. Meaning that you will be able to notice and relate to others at an entirely different level. It also transforms our perception of support. Most of us don't always need to be right, and we know that we can't always get our own way. But being truly heard and understood is what paves the way for a level of trust that allows for more mature, balanced dialogue that leads to greater alignment and acceptance.

If there is one thing you want to learn to strengthen your relationships, be better at giving feedback, to support your own team to be clearer, more connected, more decisive and more aligned, it is the art of listening. And the side benefit is you will probably find you can halve the length of all meetings, which for most leaders, would not go amiss.

3) Straight Talk

The third is straight talk. Have you ever had a conversation with someone that you were in some way fearful of having and found yourself over talking to the point where they (and maybe you) haven't a clue what you have said? What a great friend of mine, a former colleague and client Sam Sedwill, used to call pillow feedback. That is to say, a conversation suffocated and smothered by too many words. Where any silence is immediately filled with more words. Often spoken quickly and somewhat nervously. Or at the other end of the scale, where you intend to say one thing and wind up bottling it at the last minute and come out of a meeting having said nothing of what you went in to address. You talk around the subject in the hope they might perhaps, through the medium of telepathy, get it. Neither one does much good for the other person, nor does it help to resolve any issue that might need to be overcome.

Straight talk is the art of saying whatever needs to be said in short clear sentences and the ability to hold silence whilst the communication lands. Letting there be room and space for each individual to take in what is being said. This requires intention and discipline, to go as slow as is needed for real understanding to take place. Racing through it might be what you need to get it off your to do list, but effective communication of any kind can only be measured by what lands, not merely what is transmitted. Any kind of conversation that demonstrates that level of respect will be valued, even if the subject matter is not what the other person wants to hear.

I remember one conversation where I had to land feedback that the previous line manager had discussed with me on our handover, but never voiced to the individual concerned. I gave him space and the next day he came to me to tell me his wife said thank you. She had known he was stressed and unhappy for a long time, she wanted desperately for him to leave and find something that he loved so that she could have her husband back to the man he used to be. He had spent years, head down, stuck in the same role, refusing to give up. So, the feedback had helped give him the way out and the back-up she needed to help him move on. That for me was an example of mutual respect which I never forgot.

It is a great irony that when we eventually do get around to saying what needs to be said, feedback that others may have avoided, often the individual concerned at some level already knew.

As a former colleague of mine said:

"Knowing that I was never going to get to the board gave me the chance to do something different. Thank god they said it. It was a tough conversation for them to have but I had an opportunity to do something with my life. I have, and loved it."

However, I do not wish to gloss over the difficulty of giving feedback to those who genuinely do believe they have the ability and potential, where your experience would suggest otherwise. The trick is to remember that a leaders job is merely to be honest and hold a line to whatever values and behaviours you and the organisation hold dear. The reality is that whatever the individual takes from an honest conversation, and how long it takes them to really get it, is up to them.

I remember being told by an HR business partner very early in my career that I had all the innate qualities to do exceptionally well in Sales. "Marketing will frustrate you," she said. She also told me to read Vanity Fair. "You may achieve all your ambitions and realise that what you have been driving for is not what you wanted at all." I never forgot that interaction. And it took me another 15 years to truly get what she was talking about. Sales was indeed where I was happiest, being close to the customer, to the action. Where I spent my time as Sales MD leading and developing large teams of sales and service people, directly creating and implementing change at a time of great transformation, rather than in meetings, presenting upwards and dealing with the inevitable highs and mostly lows that arise with matrix management in a global structure. Shortly after getting the role I had thought I always wanted, I left what I had come to regard as a soulless endeavour.

We open, learn and change only when we are ready, and not before. But I am so glad that she said what she did. That conversation was one I never forgot. Some part of me perhaps knew that she was saying it without any other agenda than for me to be both successful and happy. Sadly, my relentless proving had to burn out first. And when it did, I knew exactly what she meant. I just wish I could remember her name to thank her now.

The very worst we can ever do is make what we see as other people's 'denial' (and our own avoidance) an excuse. Where this is the predominant driver, the cost can be significant.

As two contributors said:

"Feedback to [those lacking in self-awareness] is the hardest. Some have felt relieved whilst others have been genuinely shocked because Policing doesn't have a great pedigree of honest conversations. It happens far less now but we still suffer from those who have been 'promoted out of harm's way' – which normally means promoted so they become someone else's problem."

"I work within a Government department. And it is contradictory as honesty is so important to the organisation. But you give someone feedback and they go to the policy, they will then look at bullying and harrassment, then you get a grievance. I have had 2 already this year."

And it is sadly not uncommon:

"We have known about the attitude issues in all these people for years," said one senior leadership team I was working with, "we have just never done anything about it. We have moved them around, and just passed on the problem rather than deal with it." On the surface such behaviour can seem well intentioned: "they weren't set up for success in this role," "we didn't support them enough," "they were working for x who wasn't a great leader and we need to give them a chance." Some of which may of course be true, but if a pattern emerges where there are a large number of people who, in spite of jumping from role to role over many years, continue to display behaviours that do not fit with the expectations of the culture, that no-one has called out and dealt with, then it probably isn't anything to do with the support they are getting but an issue a little closer to home. Holding up the mirror and providing challenge is support, when done with purpose and compassion. And it is my direct experience working alongside the Chief Officer team within the Fire Service that grievances can be curtailed in the most process driven of cultures, when open and honest conversations start to happen and are role modelled with integrity and care, right from the very top.

"One of the biggest issues we have with regard to feedback has been the lack of it, and we have struggled to coach vs. just telling people what to do. But we have made significant progress. We hardly get grievances now. A habit had been formed which was adversarial, that where you encounter a problem you escalate immediately to a grievance. It speaks volumes to the loss of connection, trust in the relationship between individual and organisation if the only way to have your voice heard is through a grievance. We have broken that habit through greater confidence and trust, and people now see it is better to resolve it locally if they can. You have the opportunity to genuinely create a win win."

Straight talk is another skill to sharpen in meetings to support greater clarity, and to ensure teams get to the point, far quicker. Some people do find headlining easier than others. You may know of leaders you work alongside who have a certain verbosity, who make the same point over and over at length, who at times you may have silently, and slightly ungenerously, wondered if they merely like the sound of their own voice. That of course is a judgment, they may just find it easier to say their thoughts out loud in order to get clear themselves, but quality over quantity in all things is a truism worth remembering. Particularly when leading a team, if you have a purpose to support clarity and effective communication and allow everyone in the room to have a voice so that you get the very best result, then it really is something to pick up on. Allowing one or two people to dominate with lengthy speeches has a tendency to shut everyone else down. If you can think of meetings when this regularly happens you will notice others start to check out. Resentment will start to build towards those who take over, and the leader who does nothing to prevent it happening. Then comes apathy, as people will not be able to help but wonder why on earth they bother turning up. The aim becomes to get through the meeting, as participation in it is not in reality required. This does very little for the health of the team, or get the best result by leveraging all talent around the table. If over-talking is something you know you do yourself then make a conscious purpose in any conversation to invite the perspective of others, to actively listen to what they say. Try writing down your thoughts to get them out before you make a point and proactively welcome a prompt if you go on a bit. You and the team will not only operate better, they will respect you more for it.

4) The Question of Questions:

This is another interesting aspect contained within the art of building trusting relationships, particularly ones where you do want to get the best out of people. Much like with listening, there are different types of questions and it pays to have some consciousness over which we fall back on.

And whose benefit they actually serve.

Closed questions: these ones are easy and elicit a very simple yes or no response. Over-use of the closed question can lead a conversation into dead end or make the other person feel like they are under some kind of interrogation. So it depends on your purpose. If it is to clarify a decision or get someone who can be a little cagey and elusive off a fence, then closed questions are rather useful. But if you want to open people up then use sparingly.

Open questions: often used by salespeople and interviewers who are trained to avoid the pitfalls of the above. Open questions get people talking about themselves. They are expansive, they facilitate a dialogue, they will bring forward information and encourage disclosure. But there is a slight caveat, between open questions that are fact finding where the benefit is for you, i.e. there is something you want to know or gain from the other person opening up, and open questions that are genuinely exploratory, where the benefit is mutual, we not I. Consciousness of the purpose of the conversation will drive the quality of the outcomes from it. Lack of it can drive a jar with people, they will wonder why you are asking, start to get defensive without really knowing why (think about the last time someone cold called and started asking how you are and what you have been doing today). Purpose is everything and being explicit about why you are asking the question can help put people at ease enough to truly open, if that is indeed what you want, for them or you.

Leading questions: the question that looks open but is in fact closed. Because we have already decided what the answer is or should be. A question that in some way has an agenda attached to it. This is the kind that makes people feel that there is a right or wrong answer. Whether or not you mean to ask as a leading question is important, but you will be able to tell if the other person responds with an inflexion in their tone that suggests they are trying to please, get it right or match whatever they think is already in your head. Or they close down because there appears to be a judgment attached to the leading question, where something bad might happen if they give the 'wrong' answer. Any suggestion of control or retribution and, generally speaking, others will close down, say less or hide the truth. That alone is a good enough reason to not use a leading question but if you do catch yourself doing it there is always time to reframe and make a statement rather than a question, which is usually enough to open dialogue up in a way that has more integrity.

Socratic questions: true coaching questions are the most sought after and admired quality in leaders who coach. These are the kind that support new thinking, explore underlying beliefs and challenge assumptions, which help facilitate the release of emotion, of new ideas and approaches. Socratic questions are purposeful in that they are asked for no other reason than to support the individual or the group. There is no agenda whatsoever other than to stimulate thinking. And what is usually helpful is that there has been a conscious use of power set in the relationship between the individual asking the question and the one answering it. In other words, there is an inherent trust, the individual knows that the question is being asked for their benefit and they are in charge of what they do with the revelations, new ideas or solutions that come from the conversation. Within the context of coaching and/or traditional mentoring relationships especially where you are using an external expert, the conscious use of power and boundaries around confidentiality are hugely important and usually explicitly set. Challenges can arise with traditional leadership structures, where there is an investment in the outcome or performance, and an attachment to specific ideas (especially your own). And where, as a leader, you are ultimately assumed to be in control of all decisions and activity of those in your function or reporting line. But this is the genius of Teal organisations who break that implicit assumption and practice, through the use of internal facilitators and coaches whose purpose is to safeguard the health of the team but not control the outcome.

The intentional use of people skilled in the art of asking really great questions, purely to support the team and individuals to work at their best, is something I have seen work in an organisation that was in many ways firmly led in an Orange paradigm. In my twenties I was working as a brand manager and was hand-picked with a small number of colleagues from Marketing to be trained over several years to a high level in the art of innovation facilitation. The higher purpose was to change the culture of the organisation, to be a world-leading innovator in drinks, to challenge a marketplace and a mind-set which, up to the point of monopolies and mergers legislation, had driven growth through acquisition and vertical integration. And of course, there is no better stimulus for growth and change than when you can no longer rely on all of your previous means of controlling and dominating a market and getting what you want. A hard limit forces fresh thinking, a choice to diversify, to find another way. Or consciously choose which of the rules of the game play to your strengths and which do not, what you want to develop to promote success and what, if anything, needs to be challenged. The program of up-skilling, of embedding new innovation practices and opening up the mind-set of the marketing team was, looking back, pretty ground-breaking. One that had huge personal and company-wide benefits that resonated in the 15-20 years or so after it began. Many of the team who went through that original training to become 'Impactors' I am still in touch with, and like me, used what they had learned in ways that went far beyond the brand teams and the new product, packaging and category development that had been our original focus. Most went on to work in HR, led innovation and leadership mind-sets training internally and worked as I did as a much sought-after internal facilitator across all functions, leading transformation teams and working on integration projects. A few of us, upon leaving the organisation, still practice those skills and the art of asking great questions and stimulating new thinking for a living.

What made it ground-breaking on reflection is because it was the first training I had ever undertaken that was truly purposed to liberate and unleash the power of the team, of our individual and collective thinking and the possibilities this could create. It was purposeful, trusting, open and socratic which was quite unlike other development I had experienced up to that point (as a sales person, a graduate or a senior manager) which were mostly designed to set standards, and lay out the formula for success required by the organisation. Sell like this, present like this, manage like this, the 'insert company name here' way. Highly structured, process led trainings that suggest there is one way, with an explicit expectation that you must do it this way, 'our way' to be here and get on.

Innovation facilitation works in opposition to this mind-set, it has a light touch and does not seek to tell or teach. The process and outcomes do not work to the agenda of the facilitator, who seeks not to lead the conversation or ideas where they think it should go. It opens a space where the group has the power to step forward. A space where it is safe to take down the walls of constraint, both real and imagined. A space that supports teams to push past and step out of 'business as usual' modes of thinking and to act using the art of powerful questions, introducing stimulus which allows teams to reflect on their own learnings and seek out what can be learned from the best practice of others. The training was delivered in a way that was low on process, high on attention to behaviours and the power of experiential methods, where we learnt through doing and practice rather than theory.

That training taught me techniques that would forever change the way I engaged with, led and supported others at work during this phase of my corporate leadership career. It taught me how to lead purposeful, engaging, clearly actionable conversations that allowed others to truly step change their thinking. These conversations and the outcomes they drove to were never predictable, but the foundations of how to prepare and lead myself were. And I still use them now.

My youngest daughter Amy, bright, creative and rarely shy of using her power (and her voice) from a very young age, is perhaps the only person not to have appreciated these skills. "Mum don't use your coaching thing on me," she would say with irritation. Although it is not without a wry smile that I can confirm that 17 years of practising listening, straight talk, open and honest conversations about anything and everything have paid off. She and her sister have mastered the ability to communicate clearly and powerfully, to say what they want, and are exceptionally adept at spotting dramas. She may not have always appreciated it, but she has mastered a skill to complement her innate strengths that will serve her well in her relationships with others at home and at work.

But god help anyone who messes her about.

Reflection Exercise 5:

What feedback have you received that you recall as being the most pivotal of your career?

What do you most regret not saying? How could you use the techniques above to clear up anything that you are holding back from saying now?

Pick a relationship at work or a specific team meeting you would like to improve. Using the 6Cs in Chapter 5 as a reference for your preparation, which would help you to facilitate a better outcome?

How might you use the 4 skills and practices above (listening, questioning, straight talk, recognition of strengths) to see how you can approach this relationship or meeting differently?

Chapter 7: Taking action and getting support

"Do or not do, there is no try."

The Empire Strikes Back

I could not help but put a Yoda quote in at this point. A former client used to call me that because it was the one thing I used to say to him repeatedly; that knowing lots of theory, generating lots of possibilities, setting great intentions is all very well but if we can't execute and take the next step we are unlikely to get very far. Having opened up new perspectives, seen the issue through a different lens, looked at alternative options, this is where the rubber hits the road: what you now want to do? And when will you do it?

Want is key. If you have a clear purpose by now and are excited to try out a new technique you will. If the mind is still whirling with all the reasons why you can't, then be honest about that.

This is the filter at work, the mind's never-ending stream of narrative that goes on in all of our heads, giving us all the justifications as to what we can, cannot, should or should not do, say or be. If you have ever tuned into it, it will read like a list of excuses (mixed in with a few accusations) which at first glance appear to be fact. But the filter is worth checking, preferably with someone else you trust to be honest, as to how much of it is actually true.

A good example of this is the question I asked all of my clients: how would you rate yourself as a coach? They pretty much all gave themselves a 2 (on the grounds that they had never been formally trained) or a very British 3 out of 5. That is common, and why when facilitators ask you to rate a session between 1-10, the insightful ones will not let you rate a 7, because that's where people will default to. It's the safe option, not too high, not too low, it means you don't stand out or have to put yourself out there for other peoples' judgment. Knowing the clients I serve, I would have put them far higher in truth but again that is common too; we can be our own harshest critics.

Some did have the confidence to rate themselves a 4 or 5, and the ones that did qualified it by saying they knew their own coaching had heightened by being coached. They were now finding themselves proactively wanting to pass on what they had learnt to use themselves. Sharing learning, experience and the frameworks we know work to support others in ways that have helped us over time is indeed a very good signal that we have become consciously competent and, importantly, more confident. And when this becomes second nature, something we do with ease, it tends to get noticed by others.

So, if at this point you have a question about your own capability then go ask some people who will have a good view of the impact and influence you have, to give you some very honest feedback using the 6 Cs as a start point if that helps. If you want it, go ask for support, be coached. There really is no better way to learn that to go through the process oneself, to be in a position of openness to exploration, of vulnerability to not knowing, of understanding and mastering our own mindset and attitude. Working on ourselves and putting what we learn into practice builds competence and credibility. It is in the practice that we are able to find ways of making what at first may not seem natural, work with our strengths and in doing so, get to learn more about our limitations (real or imagined). Both will help others to be honest about their own. All of which are essential for building trust.

This really is the purpose to hold onto—of working the skills and behaviours flexibly. Not to a set formula or trying to copy someone else's style. That will always feel false to you, and to everyone else, which also gets in the way of trust.

Is there a solid framework or process that makes leading a coaching conversation easier? Yes of course. As with all else, simplicity is key, and you can't really go wrong with GROW: a coaching model developed by Sir John Whitmore, which provides a clear, practical framework for open and honest conversations that lead to new thinking, and importantly, new ways of doing and being.

GROW stands for Goal, Reality, Options, Will.

The trick is to not stick too rigidly to the process. You want people to feel that they are in a conversation that flows naturally. That you can start wherever the conversation and that individual needs to start (it is about them and not about you, or your agenda) safe in the knowledge that you can go back and forth as you would a gear system if you wish. As you look back at the concepts and exercises we have covered so far, we have followed this process. Not slavishly or sequentially, but ultimately it all ends with a 'so what?' What, as a result of what you have now reflected on, do you actually want to do differently?

I have outlined some basic questions which may help (they can also be found as a PDF on my website). Details are in the reflection exercise at the end of this chapter.

Goal

- What would you like to achieve?
- What do you want that is different to now?
- What does success/great look like?
- How will you know you have achieved it?
- How can you measure it?

Reality

- What is happening right now?
- When and how is it happening?
- What is the real issue?
- What impact does this have?
- Who else is involved?
- What is their perception of the situation?
- What have you tried so far?
- What have the results been?

Options

- What could you do to change the situation?
- What alternatives are there to that approach?
- What approaches have you seen others use that work?
- Who might be able to help?
- What are the benefits and downsides of each option?
- Which option do you propose to take forward?

Will

- What will you commit to doing?
- What you are your next steps?
- When are you going to start?
- How committed are you to taking this action?
- What might get in your way?
- What support do you need?
- When will you enlist that support?

You will, in all likelihood, know there are questions in the above you gravitate to and perhaps some which you avoid.

A client of mine sent me a great article called Prozac leadership and the limits of positive thinking written by David Collinson of Lancaster University Management School. It is well worth a read, but in essence, it speaks to the 'bring me solutions, not issues' style of leadership. In the metaphorical sense, Prozac is used to symbolise how excessive positivity can resemble an additive drug that can mitigate critical reflection. Where the pursuit of relentless optimism, or 'bright siding' can lead to a refusal to even look at unpleasant possibilities, which when planning and forecasting for major initiatives can lead to executives over inflating benefits and wildly underestimating costs or potential risks. Any organisation which rewards what could be described as optimism bias and discounts any challenge as pessimism effectively rules out the capacity to think critically (and silences committed but concerned employees in the process). Typical Prozac leadership mantras become "I only want to hear positive news," and "Bring me solutions not problems," which can have a disastrous impact on the people looking up. Firstly, it encourages positive impression management practices (those who say what they think the leader wants to hear, rather than what they truly think). Secondly, it means that genuine blocks do not get the airtime to be creatively resolved, capability is stifled and the response when risks become a reality, be they competitive, market or customer, woeful. As the author says with stunning simplicity, "Bright siding can leave organisations blind-sided."

So if we are only prepared as leaders to set goals but not look at the reality of where we are and the warning signs starting to emerge, or only look at options without wishing to explore what might support or get in the way of them happening, then we undermine our ability to move forward to achieve those goals (at best) and invite failure (at worst).

Conversations that lead to committed action are grounded in reality. The more honest we can be, the healthier we can be as individuals, as teams and as organisations. The clearer we are about what gets in the way of something happening, the easier it becomes to overcome.

As an aside, acclaimed author, Sophie Sabbage has talked about this in the book The Cancer Whisperer about her own experience of being diagnosed with Stage 4 'terminal' cancer back in 2014 with multiple tumours in her lungs, lymph nodes, bones and brain. She was 48 years old.

"I wanted to scream every time positivity was prescribed. My daughter was just four and I'd been warned I might not see her fifth birthday. I was shell-shocked and grief-stricken. Yet I found myself buffeted by a storm of imperative optimism that denied me the right to feel fear or sorrow – to be human in this most vulnerable circumstance. If I could not sit in the darkness in my darkest hour, then when?

Under what circumstance was it OK to not be OK? Even the Macmillan nurse at the hospital hurried over when I was crying in the crowded oncology waiting room, spilling her own anxiety on to my lap as she asked, 'Are you OK? Are you OK?' At this point I was riddled with tumours and terrifying symptoms. Crying seemed entirely congruent with my situation. I was fine with it. Consequently, as I looked at the dry eyes and stiff upper lips all around me, I calmly replied, 'I think I might be the only person here who is.'"

She is still thriving and her TED talk "How grief can help us win" is well worth watching for the consequences of resisting loss and of relentless positivity. It is also a beautiful testimony to what is possible when we face into reality, to win, even when we lose.

Reflection Exercise 7:

Should it be helpful, I have created a one-page summary of the GROW framework. This is available as a PDF on my website:

https://headandheartleadership.co.uk/g-r-o-w/

As we draw to a close:

Which of the key messages and concepts stand out to you?

What is your next step?

When will you do it?

Chapter 8: Summary

"The intuitive mind is a sacred gift and the rational mind is a faithful servant. We have created a society that honours the servant and has forgotten the gift"

Einstein

I love this quote. It speaks to the balance between the rational and the emotional. Between doing and being, process and behaviours. Between the tangible, all that can be seen and measured, and what lies in the realm of energy, intuitive knowing that comes from reading the situation, and how we and others feel. To the dynamics at play, underpinning relational connection, or disconnection:

- **Power and control** - Do I have a say in what happens around here?
- **Care and closeness** - Do you care about me? Do you have my back?
- **Respect and recognition** - Am I valued? Does my contribution matter?

And I think this goes to the heart of what is often absent, a blind spot rather than a conscious, deliberate omission. Where the balance to process has tipped too far, not because behaviours are not seen as important, but because over reliance is placed on one way of leading, aligning and organising people to get things done. Where control is prioritised, even if it is at the expense of people, their capability and the results they create. Or, indeed, unbounded consumerism is prioritised even if it is at the expense of our environment and our ability to sustain life on this planet. Balance in all things.

What I hope to have given you as the reader is an opportunity to reflect on our collective development over time, and the patterns of thinking and behaving that naturally emerge when we seek to organise ourselves in any system to get things done. The issues that arise in how we relate to each other when the dynamics of power, care and respect are in some way compromised or simply not attended to. The strengths and weaknesses, ways of working, structures and practices that tend to manifest depending on the underlying assumptions, beliefs and values we collectively hold about what is right, what is fixed, what is a priority; who matters and what, as a result, we can or cannot let go of. In my experience, knowing who we are, understanding where we have come from and playing to our strengths tends to be a winning strategy for individuals as much as it is organisations. This is what awareness and alignment drives: clarity and connection. A combination which unlocks an energy that supports flow. High levels of productivity that feel very easy, no matter how challenging the context might be.

What I also hope comes through is that there is no right way, no one way of doing anything. The context can change dramatically, as it has at the time of writing, in ways that could not have been imagined. What this hard stop for us all has forced is a space for creativity, for simplicity. An opportunity to think about matters most. To seek out ways we can learn, improve, adapt, evolve or indeed reinvent. In what we stand for, who we care about, what we do, what we don't do and no longer want to, when restrictions lift. This is happening for us all, both individually and collectively, and I suspect nothing will be the same now that it has. A business review on Radio 4 as we emerged out of lockdown noted two things that may now spark change for our organisations: one driven by the requirement to address the fragilities exposed (in business models, global supply chains, over reliance on imported goods driven by low cost) and greater meaningful connection to environmental sustainability and employee wellbeing. One a response to pain, one from a vision of possibility, both essential for any transformation.

Use of power is, I hope, one to reflect on. To notice the energetic difference between power (within) and control (over). Power that evokes freedom and connection, that encourages both ourselves and others, to step forward, to have a voice, to give, to create, to work at our best, more of the time.

Power that encourages us:

- to lead with more confidence and presence
- to support those we work alongside to feel a greater sense of ownership
- to create a culture that facilitates and celebrates creativity and collaboration

The practical skills I have outlined are ones we can all practice, no matter what the situation or organisational paradigm we find ourselves in. In my experience, these skills are universal and once mastered reap benefits in all areas of our lives.

The art of listening, asking purposeful questions, of straight talk—communicating with consciousness, clarity and simplicity—these aren't things we have to pull out of the bag at appraisal time, or when we are formally coaching someone in a 121. Particularly when we think about how much they matter, their purpose and role in:

- Building trusting relationships
- Facilitating greater collaboration, critical thinking, creativity, challenge and support
- Stimulating fresh thinking, new behaviour, and outstanding results

These are skills that unlock the energy for action whether that be in groups or 121, work or home. Mastering them is up to us, as the saying goes, to practise until it becomes our practice.

But what underpins all transformation in behaviour is mindset. Mindset that is driven by our sense of purpose and our beliefs. I outlined at the beginning the beliefs I hold about what drives success which sit at the heart of this book (and through this process you may have started to reflect and write your own):

Trust

Trust is the foundation. An awareness of how trust can be built and lost—how when present, this most intangible of assets is worth its weight in gold. Knowing that people give more, create more, stay longer, and spend more. It matters not whether you are looking at employees, customers or suppliers: trust has a multiplier effect when it comes to both inputs and outputs. Service, productivity and profitability are on average higher in companies with high trust scores. Where the people working in such organisations are happier, clearer and more connected to each other and their reason for existing.

Alignment

Know who you are. Through greater awareness and understanding, particularly of the organisational culture, its origins and history. Of the people that make it what it is, how they show up on the inside with each other and on the outside to customers and consumers. To members of the public who call on their services and stakeholders operating in their legislative, environmental, political and competitive contexts. Alignment only comes from a willingness to listen, notice, observe both what is said and not said, but undeniably there. To hold oneself and others in alignment, clear on who we are, what we stand for, and how this links to what we say and do.

Responsiveness

Go with what is there. Having an awareness of the tensions at play, and the ability to move with fluidity and agility. To not get fixed in one style of leadership, or indeed one mode of thinking, doing or behaving if that is not what the context or the team is calling for (or indeed, what is working).

Simplicity

Less is more. Simplicity supports good open and honest two-way communication. It helps us to take in, interpret and take action. The frameworks I use are simple, and they work in practice, which is what matters.

Realness

Realness has depth. Story telling has resonance when spoken with raw honesty, as it reminds us that we are not alone with the challenges, thoughts and experiences we face. Sharing also builds collective learning. Through practical experience, trial and error, which is the very essence of all innovative and creative practice. I hope some of the real stories and the insights contained within them serve to inspire and ignite a desire to seek out ways to make you and the relationships you have at work stronger, and the results you dare hope for that much more likely.

Encouragement

Be 'for' others. We all have the capacity to simply tell others what to do (usually with an edge of frustration), or to employ the even more short-term strategy of doing it for them. The word encouragement means to give confidence or hope, to inspire with words or behaviour, and refers to any action designed to make something more likely to happen. It is derived from the old French *corage*, meaning to give heart to another. As a mindset it is enabling, supportive, designed to liberate others to think and act with freedom and confidence. Fostering independence, not dependency.

Mindset can change anytime we choose. This is the ultimate power we all have. To own what is within our gift. To set an intention, to take a next step. If there is one you are committed to taking, having read this book, I wish you the very best. If you would like to take up some of the additional support available, details are below. And as always, I would welcome you sharing what you learn.

Further resources:

To access and download tools/frameworks to support greater confidence and capability leading with a Mindset of Encouragement please go to

Organisational Mindset:

https://headandheartleadership.co.uk/organisation al-mindset/

G.R.O.W. Model:

https://headandheartleadership.co.uk/g-r-o-w/

To discuss any aspect of executive coaching, facilitation, team diagnostics, 360 feedback on engaging leadership and coaching leadership (6Cs) or leadership development of the mindsets and skillsets outlined in *The Mindset of Encouragement* please contact nic@headandheartleadership.co.uk

Courage, dear heart. How to: look back, learn and leap forward is available on Amazon

Finally, if you wish to share your review of *The Mindset of Encouragement,* please go to Amazon. Your feedback really makes a difference.

The Mindset of Encouragement

Quick Links (Linktree)

Acknowledgements

To Mum for waking up one morning having dreamt of the title for this book. Your intuition is your super-power, and fitting that you would be the one to capture its essence exactly.

To Skyla Grayce for helping me to shape my vision a year ago. Enjoy the first book, you said. Don't rush to write the second. You were right about that. Lockdown provided the perfect moment, and when I dusted off the vision we created, I knew I was ready to go. **https://www.skylagrayce.com**

To my editor, Louise Crane and marketing consultant, Tarah Gear for reading the first draft, I am certain the second is better for your feedback. Could not have two better people to help me to do what I cannot anywhere near as brilliantly as you. **https://www.completebusinessbureau.co.uk/**

https://www.linkedin.com/in/tarahhewitt/

To James Crisp for always being there to help bring my words and concepts to a format which is simple, clear and clean. **https://www.crisp-design.co.uk**

To Mark Pringle @moreexcellent for the spark that was ignited during our creative days writing the Coaching Programme.

https://www.linkedin.com/in/mark-pringle-114750/

To Atarangi Muru and Pineaha Murray for your generosity and support. And for showing me the powers that lie in the realms in between.

https://www.maorihealers.com

https://www.thegatekeeper.nz

And to the teachers, thinking partners and coaches I have sought out over these past 8 years who have been there to guide, encourage and laugh as I found my way, and purpose.

https://www.interchange-tomo.com/art-of-hosting

https://www.waddingtonbrown.co.uk

https://wrpartnership.com

To my clients and former colleagues for their honesty and contributions for both *The Mindset of Encouragement and Courage, dear heart*. Sharing your wins and challenges have helped so many other leaders with their own. I am proud of you, and to work alongside you.

To Ella, Amy, Jack and Mark. Lockdown was always going to be memorable. You have all made it magical.

Bibliography

Shine, E. invisible forces of culture (2010) Organizational Culture and Leadership. The Jossey–Bass Business & Management Series

Laloux, F (2014) *Reinventing Organizations: A Guide to Creating Organizations Inspired by the Next Stage of Human Consciousness* | Nelson Parker

BBH Marketing Briefing (March 2020)
https://www.bartleboglehegarty.com/latest

Dr Abramson, A.
https://www.alexisabramson.com/generations/

Esther Perel article *"Where should we begin?"*
https://www.estherperel.com

Lencioni, P. M. (2002) The Five Dysfunctions of a Team: A Leadership Fable *(J–B Lencioni Series)* | Jossey Bass

Redfield, J (1994) *The Celestine Prophecy* | Bantam Books

Collinson, D. (2012) *Prozac leadership and the limits of positive thinking* | Lancaster University Management School research paper

Sabbage, S. (2016) *The Cancer Whisperer: How to Let Cancer Heal Your Life* | Hachette UK

GROW: (Sir John Whitmore, Coaching for Performance: the principles and practice of coaching and leadership | Nicholas Brealey Publishing; 5 edition (7 Sept 2017)

Open Space Facilitation Toke Moeller https://www.artofhosting.org

Nic Crisp

www.headandheartleadership.co.uk

facebook.com/headandheartleadership

instagram.com/headandheartleadership

www.linkedin.com/in/niccrisp

The Mindset of Encouragement is the second in the Head and Heart Leadership Series.

My first book was published in Feb 2019, *Courage dear Heart. How to look back, learn and leap forward* and is available to buy on Amazon.

"When we know who we are, what we want and why, ideas and action become inevitable. When the head and heart are aligned, energy shifts and momentum is created to actually do something, however small, that will propel us forward to achieve all that we want. I am a mother, consultant, facilitator, exec coach, open water swimmer and lifelong lover of people, travel and learning. In my first book I distil insights from my own experience and those of my clients in driving alignment that unlocks energy for action, with practical tools and steps to support anyone standing on the edge of change. *Courage, dear heart: How to look back, learn and leap forward* navigates the waters from a wake-up call to the moment where action becomes inevitable. So, for anyone who has a dream unfulfilled or who wants to lead others to theirs, this book is for you."

What readers say:

5.0 out of 5 stars <u>Great practical advice delivered with emotion</u>

5.0 out of 5 stars <u>An introspective guide to achieving what you want</u>

5.0 out of 5 stars <u>This is a great read - full of real life stories with practical exercises</u>

5.0 out of 5 stars <u>Just the dose of courage I needed!</u>

5.0 out of 5 stars <u>A great book for reflection and forward planning</u>

Having started Courage, dear heart I now understand why people started the Allen Carr book and then put it down before finishing it. I was scared of what I was being asked of myself. I must say at this point, the book is not scary at all... Nic holds your hand right through the whole process and there are many reflections that I am sure are universal and will be recognised by most. It has, to date, been the most challenging books I have ever read (I did go back and finish it...honestly!!) so my advice is, buy it and jump right in... just be prepared to be challenged. Big time!!

What can I say other than thank you Nic for everything. A little over a year ago I never thought today would have been possible, I was drowning in work, being a mum and seemingly failing at all of it. A short period of coaching coupled with the backup of your book really changed my 'brand'. I went from being in the throes of leaving an organisation I loved to realising the value I brought, so much so I have recently achieved my dream job managing a team. Beyond that I have coached a few others along the way and sent a few people this book. The exercises are so practical and worth referring back to, I still separate fact from opinion and check which 'box' I'm in regularly. The best bit is people have noticed, people ask all the time you are so different, how did you do it? Thank you again, I can now look forward to a great future.

For anyone standing on the edge of change, this book is for you. Insightful, honest and practical, this book offers guidance and support in so many ways. Asking some tough, but necessary questions, you will have to face truths that you may have been ignoring but I promise you, the book will leave you relieved and with clarity of mind. I cannot recommend this enough. Thank you Nic!

Nic I totally love your book. I first read this book when it was hot off the press and I was at a crossroads in my career - facing a huge decision - to stick or twist! A gamble that would affect me and those I love. I carried your book in my bag with me every day with the spine facing up. The title "Courage, Dear Heart" was there peeking at me, nudging me on every time I dipped my hand in - usually at the end of a long day just before my hideous commute that would delay me from being with my friends and family even longer! Well, I found the courage, made the plan and made the move! Life is definitely on the up! Your message was the friendly kick up the backside I needed and the guiding hand to hold while I did it! I'm now reading this again, more slowly and calmly and without the frantic rush for help that I needed last time. This time I'm taking the time to review other areas of my life that need some nurturing. So ... I wonder what else I could do if I knew I couldn't fail? Can't wait to find out. I'm definitely going to do more of what I love and a few new things too.

I brought a copy of this book for myself, I read it in 2 sittings and took action as a result. I then brought two copies for friends who also read it very quickly and took action as a result. I highly recommend it for its wisdom, comfort, practical steps and clear calls to action.

This is a great book for anyone interested in learning how to become the best version of themselves through recognising, understanding and overcoming fear. It would be especially helpful for anyone in middle to senior management who is focused on promotion and feel deep down that there may be a better way to achieve their goals, while also paying attention to what they sacrifice. The author is surprisingly honest and shares many personal stories which must have taken a lot of bravery, but the book is so much more authentic for it. This was a compelling and easy read - I read it in two sittings - and would recommend it for anyone interested in developing themselves or others.

ISBN-13: 9798670461757

Printed in Great Britain
by Amazon

bar

46282256R00138